# PRAISE

*Fearless, Fabulous You!*

"Melanie Young continues her 'Fearless, Fabulous' crusade, following on the heels of her award-winning, first book, *Getting Things Off My Chest: A Survivor's Guide to Staying Fearless & Fabulous in the Face of Breast Cancer*. Melanie's latest guide book helps the reader 'reenvision' their life, face change, and find balance and harmony within themself as the author herself did after hitting rock bottom . . . and then reclaiming her life to emerge a healthier, happier woman. The 'new' Melanie is a true inspiration, a joy to behold and totally fearless and fabulous!"

—Patrice Tanaka, author of *"Becoming Ginger Rogers . . . How Ballroom Dancing Made Me a Happier Woman, Better Partner, and Smarter CEO*

"Melanie's advice makes sense and gets me smiling. This book guides you in why it's important to get active in life—especially with reworking attitudes and finding the happiness inside of everything."

—Dr. Martha Eddy, CMA, RSMT, founder of Moving for Life

"Change is the only constant in life. Melanie Young's *Fearless, Fabulous You!* is simply brilliant! She offers a concise yet comprehensive framework to evaluate your life. Melanie's simple, yet sage suggestions can help you to create balance in your otherwise chaotic world. By letting go and 'being the change' you can create the life you desire."

—Beth Baughman DuPree, MD FACS, ABIHM, author of *The Healing Consciousness: A Doctor's Journey to Healing*, medical director of the Breast Health Program for the Holy Redeemer Health System, adjunct assistant professor of surgery at the University of Pennsylvania

## Other Books by Melanie Young

*Getting Things Off My Chest: A Survivor's Guide to Staying Fearless & Fabulous in the Face of Breast Cancer*

**Winner of the 2014 International Book Award on Cancer Health Topics**

"Owner of a wine and food marketing and special events business, Young was diagnosed with breast cancer in 2009. She employs her skills as a traveler (studying guidebooks), event planner (making lists), business-woman (noting the bottom line), and a human being (knowing when to be strong and when to ask for help), along with a healthy dose of humor, to cover the steps involved in approaching the disease and creating a plan to get through it. Lots of details and solid advice."

—*Library Journal Review*, Bette-Lee Fox, August 30, 2013

"If you know anyone that is facing breast cancer, run, do not walk, and purchase this for them! Written by a survivor, using other survivors' experience, and a healthy dose of humor, Ms. Young has written *the* go-to book for breast cancer awareness. Anything, and everything, a patient needs to know is inside, and written in a direct, informative text, without the medical journal feel."

—*Literary R&R*, Charlene, November 3, 2013

"*Getting Things off My Chest* is a perfect way to begin one's journey through dealing with breast cancer and the process of healing. Be sure to pick up a copy as soon as you are diagnosed. You'll be glad you armed yourself with its prudent guidance and foresight in getting through the treatment of breast cancer with knowledge and dignity."

—*New Mexico Review of Books*, Suzy Caplan, July 18, 2014

# FEARLESS
## FABULOUS
## *You!*

### LESSONS on LIVING LIFE
### ON *your* TERMS

## MELANIE YOUNG
AUTHOR OF *GETTING THINGS OFF MY CHEST*

PLAIN SIGHT PUBLISHING
AN IMPRINT OF CEDAR FORT, INC.
SPRINGVILLE, UT

© 2014 Melanie Young
All rights reserved.

No part of this book may be reproduced in any form whatsoever, whether by graphic, visual, electronic, film, microfilm, tape recording, or any other means, without prior written permission of the publisher, except in the case of brief passages embodied in critical reviews and articles.

The opinions and views expressed herein belong solely to the author and do not necessarily represent the opinions or views of Cedar Fort, Inc. Permission for the use of sources, graphics, and photos is also solely the responsibility of the author.

ISBN 13: 978-1-4621-1544-0

Published by Plain Sight Publishing, an imprint of Cedar Fort, Inc.
2373 W. 700 S., Springville, UT 84663
Distributed by Cedar Fort, Inc., www.cedarfort.com

LIBRARY OF CONGRESS CATALOGING-IN-PUBLICATION DATA
Young, Melanie, 1959-author.
  Fearless fabulous you! / Melanie Young.
      pages cm
Includes bibliographical references and index.
Summary: Written for anyone who feels "stuck" and needs help to reframe their views, readjust their attitudes, and reapply their talents.
ISBN 978-1-4621-1544-0 (alk. paper)
1. Life change events. 2. Self-esteem. 3. Self-evaluation.  I. Title.

BF637.L53Y68 2014
158.1--dc23
                                2014027729

Cover design by Angela D. Baxter
Cover design © 2014 by Lyle Mortimer
Edited by Daniel Friend and typeset by Eileen Leavitt
Artwork by April Stewart

Printed in the United States of America

10  9  8  7  6  5  4  3  2  1

Printed on acid-free paper

To Sonia Young, The Purple Lady,

and David Ransom, my loving husband.

A special thank you to Bonnie Tandy Leblang.

# Contents

CONTENTS

## Reframe

## Reclaim

## Notes

One day, she remembered that the only person who could make her happy was herself! So she took back her power, re-claimed her place in the world and shined like never before.

—Anna Taylor, healer, international recording artist

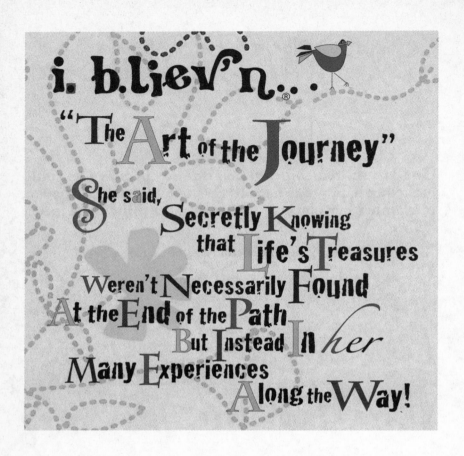

*i. b.liev'n...*

*"The Art of the Journey"* She said, Secretly Knowing that Life's Treasures Weren't Necessarily Found At the End of the Path But Instead In *her* Many Experiences Along the Way!

## AND SO SHE BEGAN—AGAIN

There was a time when I felt stuck between worlds that clashed. I asked myself, "Are my best years behind me, or are my worst years behind me? What is still to come, and what can I do to make changes for the better?" I was midway through my life in terms of age and stage, but a few curtains had closed, and I was grasping around, trying to find the openings.

I had just completed treatment for breast cancer. My father had passed away from cancer the year I was diagnosed. I marked my twentieth anniversary in business for myself by closing my public relations agency, letting my staff go, and refocusing my career as a writer and consultant. I harbored anger over my "lost year" undergoing treatment for cancer, struggling to keep afloat financially, and mourning the one person whom I counted on all my life to have my back when the chips were down: my father. I knew I did not want to go back to my old life as an overworked public relations executive. I knew that my life moving forward needed to be more balanced, less stressful, and overall healthier. I wanted to reclaim my life and live it on better terms.

I speak with women and men around the country, and they have shared their stories about feeling stuck between two worlds. Many are cancer survivors, but not all. Many have faced other challenges and changes and find themselves in transition, whether by choice or otherwise. Most have reached a point in life where they are taking stock and seeking balance and purpose. Some have been successful. Others are still finding their way.

Becoming unstuck does not happen overnight. Life is a work in progress. Like a work of art, your life needs care and maintenance. And sometimes you need to change the frame or setting to give it new perspective.

I sculpted my own mental and physical makeover like an artist. I took stock of my own life and my personal tools—my skills, talents, and strengths—and thought about ways I could repurpose them. I overhauled my mental and physical self with a healthier diet, daily exercise, meditation, and stress management. I made a list of everything I felt was good in my life and everything that I felt needed to be eliminated or changed to make things better. And when I looked at the two columns side by side, I realized I had a lot to offer. But I needed to rechannel my energy, release any negativity holding me back, and rethink my goals if I wanted to make a change. You can't retrace your steps in life, but you can choose the direction you want take moving forward.

More important, I realized I needed to kick my tires, change my mental oil, and recharge my batteries for a smoother ride down the road of the rest of my life. I may have hit a few bumps and had some parts replaced, but my engine was still running fine.

We all have the capacity to stay fearless and fabulous at every age and stage of our lives.

Don't let anyone make you think or feel otherwise. And if life hands you a few bad cards, it doesn't mean you have to fold. You need to reshuffle the deck and deal again.

Always remember: Aim to live life on your terms with passion and purpose. And always try to enjoy the ride.

Stay Fearless & Fabulous!

i. b.liev'n... #ILikeBeingMe!

"The Fine Art of Being Me!"

She said, Thinking it was All About Creating her Own Set of Rules Instead of Trying to Squeeze herself Into Someone Else's!

# Recharge

May I have the courage today
To live the life that I would love,
To postpone my dream no longer
But do at last what I came here for
And waste my heart on fear no more.

—John O'Donohue, Irish Poet
"A Morning Offering"—*Benedictus*
(To Bless the Space Between Us in the US)

# MAKE YOU A PRIORITY

*Never allow someone to be your priority*
*while allowing yourself to be their option.*
—Kelly Angard, American artist and photographer[1]

**W**hen you wake up in the morning, what is your first priority? Is it compiling a to-do list for work or running errands? Rethink that list now! Make it a "to–care" list. Start with what you are going to do to take care of yourself today, and *then* decide how you'll tackle everything else coming your way. Buying groceries, taking your kid to volleyball practice, and nailing that perfect PowerPoint presentation are tasks to accomplish. But first, take care of yourself. It's neither a task nor an accomplishment; it's a privilege.

I speak often about the importance of making *you* a priority. My attitude is this: If you don't take care of yourself, who will? Maintaining good health is your right and your responsibility. I never really liked the idea of self-sacrifice. You should never sacrifice your sense of self. Life is a gift to care for, not something to neglect or abuse.

Someone once asked me, "Aren't you being a little self-indulgent? Shouldn't you put others first as a compassionate individual?"

I responded, "Making your well-being a priority is neither selfish nor self-indulgent. It's about self-reliance and self-sustainability. How can you be present to support and help others if you don't sustain yourself first?"

For years, I worked nonstop building a successful business. My clients were my priority, and I was proud of the well-planned campaigns and events we provided and the great results we delivered. But when the economy collapsed, my clients reset their priorities and moved on. It may have been emotional for me, but not for them. As I was told over and over, "It's just business." I was not their priority, so why were they my priority?

I also put my well-being second. I skipped meals and regular exercise, allowed stress to wreak havoc on my body and my sleep, and never gave myself enough downtime to balance the workload. These unhealthy patterns caught up with me, and the tipping point was my breast cancer diagnosis in 2009. Over the years, I didn't listen to my body when I thought I was having a heart attack. I didn't listen when I started having strange skin rashes. I didn't listen when I was diagnosed with gastritis. But when my doctor delivered my cancer diagnosis, I finally sat up and listened. And the message sunk in and took hold.

I taught myself to reset my priorities. My health and well-being came first, then family and friends. I changed my diet, started exercising daily, and learned to meditate and relax and let stress roll off my shoulders rather than weigh me down. It takes discipline, but if you don't do it for yourself, who will do it for you? Instead of letting yourself go through neglect, let go of the things that are no longer healthy for you. Paying attention to *you* will only strengthen your attention to what is around you and the possibilities that lie ahead.

Taking care of your health is not only about managing what you eat. It's also about managing what's eating you. The right foods and a daily workout can only take you so far if your mind is consumed with problems and stress is causing you sleepless nights. Identify your stress trigger points and work on ways to deal with them. Are you stressed because of demands other people place on you, or is it because you place too many demands on yourself? How are you spending your energy? Are you exhausted by the end of the day or exhilarated? If you don't feel your best self, it may time to reset your priorities.

I have friends who gave up careers to focus on their family. This was their priority, and it was important. Family and friends can serve as a caring support network if doors close on you. They won't judge you by how many sales you generate or how many clients you win or lose. Instead, they'll make you laugh and forget, and they will teach you to be patient, giving, and forgiving. But even family and friends may not always be there for you. You need to rely on yourself first.

You should never lose your sense of self or make sacrifices, even for those you care about deeply, if it negatively impacts your mental and physical health and stability. Making sacrifices for those you love is fine as long as it is not self-sacrifice. Airline flight attendants tell parents to put the oxygen masks over their faces first before placing them on their children for a reason; you have to save yourself first to be able to protect your loved ones.

Making you a priority is about self-esteem. You are a worthy individual who deserves the right to take better care of yourself and be treated with respect. That is your message. And it is a significant one to share with your family, especially children, who will hopefully follow your example.

Beware of emotional knockouts and dumps. These include being too critical of yourself, allowing others to make you feel insignificant or unworthy, dumping your problems on someone else, or allowing others to dump on you. These can unsteady you and make you want to give up. You were not put on this earth to give in or give up. You were put in this world to be giving, and you were given a mind and a body to nourish and nurture—to give life. Never underestimate your worth.

> *If I am not for myself, who is for me?*
> *But if I am only for myself, who am I? If not now, when?*
> *—Rabbi Hillel, Jewish scholar*[2]

## FEARLESS FABULOUS FIVE:

1. Put your well-being first. It is not selfish; it is smart life management.

2. The most important approval you need to seek is your own. Confidence comes from caring for yourself and believing in your potential.

3. How you treat yourself sets an example for how others should treat you.

4. Taking time to take care of yourself will you give your more energy to enjoy the rest of your time.

5. While your personal and professional priorities may change over time, the priority of *you* should be a constant.

> *Be yourself because an original is worth more than a copy.*
> *—Unknown*

## TEN TIPS TO RESET AND RECHARGE

1. **Breathe**: Go outside and enjoy fresh air and recharge your mind. Exhale deeply to alleviate stress. Inhale to clear your head.

2. **Move**: Commit to at least thirty to forty-five minutes of daily exercise. Mix it up so you challenge different muscles each day.

3. **Savor**: Make smarter, healthier food choices. Focus on mindful eating and the pleasure of the meal rather than rushing.

4. **Sleep**: Make bedtime *your* time to really unwind. Your bedroom should be a relaxation chamber, not an extension of your office.

5. **Create**: Just for fun, take up a hobby that expands your mind and see where it takes you.

6. **Share**: Spend time with friends and family. Volunteer for a charity. Mentor someone. You will never know the true value of the gifts you have until you share them with others.

7. **Laugh**: Laughter lifts the spirits and reminds you to lighten up. Sometimes, you just shouldn't take things too seriously.

8. **Thank**: Gratitude is next to godliness. Everyone appreciates a solid and sincere thank-you, and few people take the time to express it.

9. **Imagine**: Look at everything with open eyes and an open mind. Avoid being overly judgmental or critical. Believe in possibilities, not impossibilities. Opinions should be free, not confining.

10. **Explore**: Try new things. Visit new places. Ask questions. Be curious. It keeps your mind young and active. Free your mind to wander and to wonder.

# KNOW THE VALUE OF YOUR SELF-WORTH

*Self-worth comes from one thing—thinking that you are worthy.*
*—Dr. Wayne Dyer, author and motivational speaker.*[1]

**T**he most important thing parents can teach their children is the importance of believing in themselves and the value of their self-worth. No matter where you go or what you do, being content with yourself and comfortable in your body will make those around you feel more at ease.

I grew up inspired by the concept of self-worth, probably because so many people tried to make me feel unworthy as I progressed through an awkward adolescence. As a high school senior, I wrote a paper on self-worth, and its message still resonates: "Self-worth can only be verified by you, your values, and your goals. Not one person's opinion of you is half as important as the one you hold of your own self."

Many people confuse self-worth with net worth or with being worthy. Not so. Money cannot buy self-worth. It's not a commodity you can trade. People can't steal your self-worth, but some may try to devalue it, usually in an attempt to make themselves feel worthier. Don't fall for it.

Self-worth is an intangible value that has very tangible outcomes. People with a strong sense of self-worth project a healthy confidence that can achieve many things. You can teach the value of self-worth to inspire others to believe in themselves. You can help empower someone to take action. You can lift the spirits of a friend whose self-worth has taken a beating.

Self-worth is not about financial income; it is about personal outcome. Once you learn to be less competitive and more compassionate, less self-critical and more self-confident, you'll gain a clearer understanding of who you are and how you want to live your life. And when you take

7

action to realize it, the value of your self-worth will increase. And *that* is priceless.

> *We must not allow other people's limited perceptions define us.*
> —*Virginia Satir, American author and psychotherapist*[2]

FEARLESS FABULOUS FIVE

1. Self-worth is about who you are, not what you have.
2. Self-worth is about the difference you make, not how much you make.
3. Self-worth is valuing yourself. Someone with a strong sense of self-worth always feels worthy.
4. Having self-worth does not necessarily mean you are self-absorbed. It means you have self-esteem.
5. If someone tries to devalue your self-worth by making you feel anything less than worthy, walk away. Self-worth is your greatest asset. Never let anyone shortchange you, and never underestimate your value in this world.

> *No one can make you feel inferior without your consent.*
> —*Eleanor Roosevelt, First Lady of the United States*[3]

# PORTION CONTROL: YOUR LIFESTYLE DIET

*I've learned that you can't have everything and
do everything at the same time.*
—Oprah Winfrey, American actress and television talk show host[1]

**P**ortion control. **It's an important step in maintaining a** healthy diet and fighting obesity. I also feel that non-food portion control is necessary for maintaining our overall health. Many of us are guilty of biting off more than we can chew, living on a steady diet of appointments and commitments served with a side dish of anxiety. Trying to fit it all in and get it all done by a deadline may not be realistic or fair to yourself or to others.

Are you guilty of having too much on your plate? Do you have an excessively long to-do list? Do you feel overloaded and overtaken by obligations? If you answered *yes* to any of these questions, it's time to go on a portion control lifestyle diet.

Like any diet, this means cutting back and making healthy adjustments. Understandably, if you're working two jobs, raising children, and caring for your home to make ends meet, learning to control your time is hard. But any diet takes determination and discipline. The goal is to improve your health and well-being, and your health and well-being must take precedence. As I have stated before, putting your well-being first ensures that you are strong for yourself and those you care about.

Gulping down your meal in a hurry isn't nearly as pleasurable as taking time to savor each bite. So why rush through your life, moving from deadline to deadline to get things done without taking time for any enjoyment? You can't live on a steady diet of overwork just as your body cannot tolerate a steady diet of overeating. Why be a glutton for self-punishment because you tried to do too much and master everything, especially to please or compete with others? Learn to lean down your daily task list, identify and trim time-wasters, and do the best you can at a pace that is right for you.

> *Once she stopped rushing through life, she was amazed*
> *at how much more life she had time for.*
> —*Amy Rubin Flett, Canadian artist*[2]

## FEARLESS FABULOUS FIVE

Like any food diet, a balanced lifestyle diet should be based on your individuality, your environment, and what you can tolerate. Here are some simple things you can do:

1.  *Nourish yourself.* All diets start with changing your attitude about what you are putting into your body. Eating fresh, wholesome, non-processed foods in moderate portions, staying well-hydrated, and ingesting the right balance of nutrients for your age and ideal body weight are all fundamentals of good health.

2.  *Nurture your body.* It is an established fact that daily physical exercise is critical to good health. The minimum recommendation is thirty minutes a day. It's as important as having regular medical checkups according to your age and medical history. Also remember to protect your skin with sunscreen and to get enough quality sleep.

3.  *Allocate your time.* Learning to manage your time is one of the hardest challenges you might face. First, shorten your to-do list. Include only those things that are absolutely essential for you to address that specific day. If the task can wait, let it. The world will not come to an end. Second, learn to say no when someone asks for more of your time. If you must commit to something new, such as a pressing work assignment, negotiate a realistic timeline and deadline to get things done. Third, set aside specific times of the day to answer emails and engage in social media. If someone really needs to reach you, they should be calling or texting you, not emailing. Fourth, learn to push the "pause button" and take a little time for yourself to reset your energy.

4.  *Cultivate your mind.* Feeding your mind is important to your mental balance. Read a book, listen to music, watch a movie, take up a hobby, play games, or work on a crossword puzzle. Be

curious and ask questions. Whatever you do, make sure your mental cultivation it is not all work-related.

5.    *Foster relationships.* There is absolutely nothing healthier than laughing with friends, playing with your kids, or cuddling up with your significant other or your pet dog or cat. I enjoy getting nearby friends together for dinner as much as picking up the phone to chat with a friend far away or dropping someone a note. It's also important to connect with yourself. Set aside time for *you* to do something you truly enjoy, whether alone or with someone who shares your enthusiasm.

> *Fear less, hope more;*
> *eat less, chew more;*
> *whine less, breathe more;*
> *talk less, say more;*
> *hate less, love more;*
> *and all good things are yours*
> —*Swedish proverb*[3]

# LESSONS BEYOND LEANING IN

*You can tell who the strong women are. They are the ones you see building one another up instead of tearing each other down.*
*—Unknown*

**L**ean in: "To incline or press into something. You have to lean into the wind when you walk or you will be blown over."[1]

Much has been said and written about Facebook CEO Sheryl Sandberg's bestselling book, *Lean In*. Some blogs referred to it as "a feminist manifesto" to motivate women in business to be assertive, set goals, establish boundaries, and speak up and out if they want to shatter the glass ceiling and establish equality between the working sexes.

As a woman and a business owner, I found her message compelling, based both on my successes and my mistakes. Here's my interpretation: It takes more than a traditional MBA—Master of Business Administration—to get ahead. It also takes a "Master of Being Assertive."

I had no formal business training when I started out, just a clear vision of what I wanted, a talent for telling a compelling story, a willingness to knock on a lot of doors, and thick skin. My higher education is a combination of a liberal arts college degree, gut instinct, and street smarts. I learned everything while establishing and running my own business and dealing with the debris that life tossed in my path. I earned a "Master of Being Assertive" on the road to success. Along the way, I learned that (unless you were born with a silver spoon in your mouth) if you want to get ahead, you need to be prepared to shovel some poop. And I learned that if you want to build your life in any direction you choose, you need to start by establishing a strong platform.

But leaning in is only part of the lesson. For any strong foundation in your business or in your life, you need to have a support system. You shouldn't try to take on everything yourself. Otherwise, you may lean too far and become unsteady. You need to be assertive but also be adaptable. You have to speak your mind but also be a good listener. You need to know when to fight for something and when to fold when it is no longer worth it. You need to be prepared to listen to your wits and your gut as well as stats and reports when you make decisions.

A FEW TIPS:

**Lean On:** Seek help or advice when you need it. It saves energy, spares you time, and can help avoid costly mistakes. This applies to both your business and your personal life. I would never prepare my own taxes and I would never cut my own hair. I am skilled at neither, so why attempt it and screw up? Focus on what you do best, and assign other tasks to people who can do it better than you. Sometimes "divide and conquer" goes much further than doing it all yourself. If you can't afford to hire someone, consider bartering services.

**Listen Up:** Listen carefully when people speak to you. It is a sign of respect. A poor listener is just as bad as an inarticulate speaker. Make sure what someone is saying to you is the same as what you are hearing so there is no misinterpretation of the message. If you are unclear on what someone is saying to you, ask them to repeat it or repeat it back to them.

Count to ten before you respond to a question. We tend to fill in blank pauses with pointless comments. A pause can be a powerful statement that you are thinking things over before you respond. Taking time to process a response also gives you time to center yourself. No one complains when someone is a good listener, but many complain when someone talks too much.

**Speak Up:** Practice speaking with a confident tone of voice and excellent grammar. If you are in a business or social situation, introduce yourself clearly. I can't begin to tell you how many people I meet who neglect to tell me their full name, even after I have told them mine. Be a good conversationalist; this means knowing how to get your point across succinctly or sharing a story that engages without dominating the discussion. Sharing your opinion is important, but let others share theirs as well. No one wants to talk to someone who refuses to listen.

**Look Out:** Look out for and be open to timely opportunities. This is important whether you want to get out of a rut, advance your career, or start something new. If an opportunity presents itself, make sure you understand the time frame you have to make a decision before someone else grabs it. Look out for yourself, but also look out for others. If an opportunity doesn't fit your needs or goals, it may be suitable for someone you know. Pass it along to friends and colleagues who will appreciate the referral.

**Lift Up:** Being mentored helps you gain knowledge, and becoming a mentor helps you share it. Be generous with encouragement and stingy with criticism. Be patient. Most people are trying and just need a hand to guide them. People ask me what I consider my greatest success. I always respond that I am most proud of the people I have trained and helped through my work.

*If you want to lift yourself up, lift up someone else.*
—*Booker T. Washington, American educator, author, civil rights activist*[2]

FEARLESS FABULOUS FIVE

1. Be assertive. Speak up, ask questions, be heard, and make your opinion matter and your presence valued.

2. Education is not always about earning degrees. It's about gaining experience.

3. Know your strengths and weaknesses and when to ask for help.

4. Be both an articulate speaker and an attentive listener.

5. Be supportive. Everyone needs a lift at some point.

*A successful woman one is one who can build a firm foundation*
*with bricks others have thrown at her.*
—*Unknown*

# BE YOUR OWN DEFINITION OF BEAUTY

*Imperfection is beauty, madness is genius, and it's better*
*to be absolutely ridiculous than absolutely boring.*
—*Unknown*

**A**cademy Award-winning actress Lupita Nyong'o gave a speech in which she revealed how, as a young girl, she prayed to God to lighten her skin. She said she was teased and taunted for her dark complexion and felt that by lightening her skin, she would be perceived as beautiful. Tears welled up in her eyes as she shared her story of believing she was ugly: "When I was a teenager, my self-hate grew worse. . . . My complexion had always been an obstacle to overcome. . . . I had begun to enjoy the seduction of inadequacy."[1]

Meanwhile, promotional ads for tanning products to make a fair woman's skin several shades darker are all over the Internet. Why should any person of color feel the need to lighten his or her skin to be beautiful—or light-skinned individuals feel the need to darken theirs with spray tans or tanning booths?

We live in an era where we preach eating natural, wholesome foods to feed our skin and stay healthy, but we turn to doctors to plump, peel, inject, and reshape us with various substances when nature turns against us. Who are really the arbiters of what determines a person's beauty, and why do we have to follow what they say? Beauty is subjective, as the phrase goes, "In the eye of the beholder." When you look in the mirror, what do you behold? Do you see only flaws, or do you see the full picture?

I was teased as an adolescent for having a skinny face and bad skin. It made me self-conscious, and for many years I would not leave my home without wearing my war paint of cover-up makeup. I underwent many painful and costly surgical and dermatological corrective procedures to

17

help me feel comfortable in my own skin. But none of that mattered until I taught myself to *believe* that I was beautiful.

I think every woman needs to learn to be comfortable in her own skin based on *her* opinion of what is beautiful, not the opinions of mass media, marketers, or society. Young girls need to be taught to love their bodies, not taunted for looking different.

Self-worth is more important than face value and *that* beauty starts from within. The first measure of being beautiful is not based on how you look to others but on how you look at yourself. The second is how you take care of yourself. Staying strong and healthy starts from the inside out. The third is compassion—how you treat others.

Ms. Nyong'o eventually came to realize this: "Beauty was not a thing I could acquire or consume. It was something I just had to be. . . . What does sustain us . . . what is fundamentally beautiful is compassion for yourself and for those around you. . . . That you will feel the validation of your external beauty but also get to the deeper business of being beautiful inside. There is no shade in that beauty."

> *Self-confidence is the most attractive quality a person can have. How can anyone see how awesome you are if you cannot see it for yourself?*
> *—Unknown*

## FEARLESS & FABULOUS FIVE

1. Define your own style or look and own it. Dress the part you want to be.

2. Never let anyone make you feel underappreciated or ugly.

3. Beauty starts from within with a conscious diet, a cared-for body, and a confident and caring attitude.

4. You cannot buy or find beauty; you have to feel it.

5. If you are not happy with yourself, you will never truly feel beautiful no matter how many beautiful things surround you.

> *She decided to see how her life would change if she dropped the assumption she needed fixing.*
> *—Amy Rubin Flett, Canadian artist[2]*

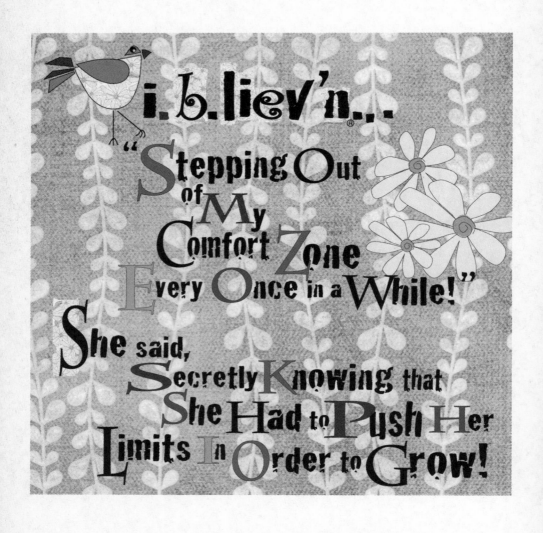

# Release

In the end these things matter most:
How well did you love? How fully did
you live? How deeply did you let go?

—Unknown

# CHANGE IS SOMETHING YOU WANT FOR YOURSELF

*Not everything that is faced can be changed, but*
*nothing can be changed until it is faced.*
—*James Baldwin, American essayist, playwright and novelist*[1]

**S**ometimes you face changes in life by choice. You want to switch careers, move cities, break off relationships, lose weight, or experience any other type of transformation. Choosing to make a change in your life for the better, especially when you are feeling stuck, is a defining moment and one that will require—and reinforce—your inner strength.

You have to understand why you want change. When I chose to close my PR agency, a company that helped define me for twenty years, I knew I was taking a risk knowing I did not have a secure plan in place for my next steps. But I also knew that not making the change would mean falling back into unhealthy work patterns and situations that I was convinced were no longer advantageous for my well-being.

Other times, you are forced to make a change. You lose your job or receive a promotion. You become ill or need to care for a loved one who is sick. Someone leaves your life, either for better or worse. When these changes happen, you have to decide how to respond. You have the option of longing for your former way of life, but you also have the option to repurpose and start fresh.

My husband likes to say, "If you want to change your life, change your residence." Others say, "Change your job" or, "Change your looks." I don't think you need to go to such drastic measures, and it may not make sense when you have family or community obligations. I'm an advocate for making the right kind of change at the right time based on your needs, desires, economic situation, and ability to patiently manage the change.

I also feel changing your location won't make a bit of difference if you bring negative emotional baggage with you.

You may want to make a change but the time is not right. You might have young children at home, a dying parent to care for, debts to pay off that require you to take a steady but unexciting job, or an unforeseen disaster could occur that is out of your control. You may need to change your point of view, take stock of what you have around you, and make the best of what you can do in the moment.

Sometimes making small changes can result in a big difference. The change can be about time, such as stepping out of a routine or adjusting your daily schedule to give yourself an extra hour a day to exercise or take up a new hobby. Change can be physical, such as getting a new hairstyle, losing weight, or restyling your wardrobe. Change can be spatial, such as rearranging your furniture, taking a new route to work, planting a garden, or painting a room.

Many people are resistant to change. They say things like, "That's how it's always been done" or, "If it's not broke, why fix it?" or, "Things are going just fine. Why rock the boat?" Many traditions are good—they provide a seamless continuity and a constructive history between past, present, and future. But resistance to a necessary or timely change is risky business. The reality is, people and situations change around us. If you're not adaptable, you can become, at least to others, irrelevant and dispensable.

It's important to make a change because it is your choice, not because someone is forcing you to change. If someone keeps pressuring you to change, and if it makes you uncomfortable, you should verbalize your concerns and reconsider the relationship. However, if someone is encouraging you to change an unhealthy habit, it is worth listening and having their support.

It is also important to consider the consequences of change. You are not the only person affected. If you decide to move, your family moves with you. If you decide to buy a dog, are you prepared to care for it? Are you emotionally and financially prepared to make a major change, like starting a family? Some changes are permanent, and some are not. Change should not be made in haste without all options and costs being considered. You can always return or exchange an article of clothing at a store, or sell a home or boat, but you can't return a child once you've decide to have a baby.

The most important change you can make is the change from a negative outlook or attitude to a positive one. If you don't make that change first, anything else you change won't make much of a difference.

*If you don't like something, change it.*
*If you can't change it, change the way you think about it!*
—*Mary Engelbreit, American author and illustrator*[2]

## FEARLESS FABULOUS FIVE

1. When you decide what you want to change in your life, write down pros and cons. Make sure you *want* to make the change and understand the reasons and consequences before you start.

2. Don't make a change to please someone else or if it makes you uncomfortable. Change should be *your* decision.

3. Change will come at a price. What are you willing to invest in terms of time and money? Acknowledge what you are willing to give up in order to change.

4. Be considerate of those around you who will be impacted by your change. Make sure they understand why things are changing, what to expect, and what you expect from them.

5. If you make a change and then regret it, remember that you can always make another change. You may not be able to go back, but you can always move in another direction.

*Your life does not get better by chance. It gets better by change.*
—*Jim Rohn, American entrepreneur, author, and motivational speaker*[3]

# LETTING GO: FALL OR FLY?

*We must be willing to let go of the life we have planned*
*so as to have the life that is waiting for us.*
—*Unknown*

**L**etting go can be one of the most painful yet healing experiences you will ever face. One of my hardest lessons in letting go was my decision to euthanize my beloved Maltese dog, Chance, who was my guardian angel for fourteen years. He was in pain, and his mind and body had been desiccated from a nasal tumor that was slowing taking over his brain. I wrestled with the idea of euthanasia. I finally realized how much I truly hated the idea of letting go of a life, particularly his. The doctors said it was my choice, but they suggested I think of it as a gift to him—a gift of peace and protection from more pain.

I realized I was keeping Chance alive because *I* was afraid of losing him without thinking of his suffering. I had to put his physical pain first and my emotional pain second. I grappled with the choice I had to make to end a life; I never realized how difficult it would be. In the end, I relented. Chance died quietly in my arms, my hand over his small chest as the last beat of his heart faded away.

As the veterinarian removed Chance from my lap and gathered his body in her arms to take him away, his tiny head flipped backward and his face looked at me. His eyes were still open in an expression that said, "I don't want to leave you, Melanie."

My heart sank. It was the same expression on my dying father's face when I told him good-bye and walked out of the hospital room, never to see him again. My father soldiered on as he marched toward his death, lingering in hospice. But I knew his mind had already let his life go; he was prepared to leave. He had told me in no uncertain words. And somehow, I was better prepared for his death because we had discussed it and accepted it.

27

I don't believe in letting go easily. I'm a bit of an emotional hoarder, and I've always viewed letting go to mean "letting down" or "giving up." I'm a Type-A personality, a go-getter and a cancer survivor. People like me aren't supposed to give up. We're supposed to face the fight head on. Letting go was a sign of weakness in my mind.

But letting go is really a demonstration of being in command of yourself. Letting go is not just about life-and-death decisions. It is about making decisions that change your life hopefully for the better. Letting go of something that is harmful or that no longer works in your life is a sign of strength. Letting go can be healthy. Relatives let go of their burdensome house and move on to a new life in a new location. Friends let go of dead-end jobs and pursue new careers or start businesses. A cancer survivor lets go of her fears and bad habits and discovers a more balanced way to live. A hoarder lets go of all the stuff in her house and finds more space to move and think. A woman whose husband has left her lets go of her anger and becomes open to meeting someone new to spend her life with. Sometimes, when *you* let someone go, they may come back—and hopefully they'll come back better.

I learned from losing Chance and my father two years earlier that, while death is an inevitable passage of life that you cannot control, you can choose how you rechannel your pain and let go of the anger. I turned to writing, which has led to my books. I am more sensitive to the pain a friend may feel when a loved one is ill.

Just as hard as letting go is being let go. Some of the most painful experiences in my life were my being dumped by boyfriends or losing longtime clients because they decided they wanted a fresh new team. The hurt and anger you feel is excruciating. But it is not worth it to allow anger to fester for too long, especially if it impacts your well-being. If someone no longer respects your value and does not want you in their life, then you might as well let them go.

Letting go emotionally can open your mind and your heart. Letting go physically can relieve pain and tension. It's about unclenching your tight fist and opening your palm for someone to hold or for you to reach out.

Letting go may seem hard, but choose to view it as setting free. Learn to release to find inner peace.

*Some of us think holding on makes us strong, but sometimes it is letting go.*
*—Hermann Hesse, German-Swiss poet, novelist, and painter*[1]

FEARLESS FABULOUS FIVE

1.  Letting go should not be viewed as letting someone down or giving up.

2.  Letting go should be viewed as a release—freeing someone or something to move onward.

3.  Letting go is not the end of the world. It can be the beginning of a new life.

4.  Letting go physically can be scary and deadly if you are hanging on a ledge or a cliff. But emotionally, letting go should be viewed as a release—a release from anger, fear, pain, burdens, or anything that balls you up and brings you down.

5.  When you let yourself go or someone you care about go, it will only make you both spread your wings and land softly on higher ground. It's like tossing seeds in the air to sprout elsewhere.

*The more anger towards the past you carry in your heart,*
*the less capable you are of loving the present.*
—Barbara De Angelis, PhD, American author and motivational speaker[2]

# 8.

# REFLECT BUT DON'T DWELL

*If you pay attention to the darkness, you will never find the light.*
—*Thomas A. Richards, PhD, American psychologist*[2]

**D**o you know someone who is stuck in the past, always talking about the "good old days"? Such people love to bring up stories about days gone by that you may have already said good-bye to and moved away from. It's not that you shouldn't enjoy looking back and reflecting, but you should make sure it's a healthy and positive reflection that doesn't cloud your present or your ability to move forward. Make up your mind to reflect on anything negative as a learning experience and on anything positive as a happy memory.

I started this book talking about a time when I wasn't sure whether my best days or my worst days were behind me. I caught myself reflecting too much on all that had been and not focusing enough on all that could be. I started to dwell on bad choices, missed opportunities, and those "good old days" that I wished to recapture. But you cannot recapture or fix the past; instead, you need to seize the present and make adjustments to better prepare for the future. I needed to learn how to release my past and the questions and doubts attached to it in order to free myself and allow myself to move on.

When bad things happen to good people, be it disease, death, divorce, or any number of deep ditches in the road of life, it can derail you for a time. But if you dwell on what has occurred for too long, you will fall into a dark tunnel of despair. Anxiety and despair are the compounded interest of dwelling too much on things that you could not or can no longer control. If you're going to dwell on something, dwell on the all options you have in your life moving forward, not on the choices you made that are now behind you.

When I was diagnosed with breast cancer, I learned to stop dwelling on what led to my diagnosis and why it happened to me. I even stopped dwelling on the year of surgeries and treatment that I endured. Instead, I focused on turning my experience into a lesson on how to take better care of myself and use the knowledge I'd acquired to inspire others do the same. Sure, there were plenty of times, post-treatment, when my mind was still adjusting to a "new normal" and I reflected on and regretted my lost year, my changed body, and the reality that I was more vulnerable than I thought.

But then I realized that dwelling on those regrets was not getting me anywhere and that I needed to refocus on the fact that I had *survived* cancer instead of losing my life to it. I needed to focus on the years ahead and not the year I had lost. And the only way this could happen was by changing my attitude. The reflection in my mental mirror needed to be more positive. The first thing I had to do was release my grief. The second was avoiding fear of recurrence, of losing another loved one, or of dying. The third was being more accepting and appreciative of myself, my new body, and the people around me.

The evil cousins to dwelling too much on the past are regret and guilt. Why bother allowing regret into your life? If you make a terrible mistake (let's call it a bad choice), you can try and correct it, or you can live with it and move on. The noun *regret*, according to *Merriam-Webster's* definition, is "a feeling of sadness or disappointment about something that you did or did not do . . . [or] sorrow aroused by circumstances beyond one's control or power to repair."[2]

The word *guilt* is associated with wrongdoing. Sometimes you have done nothing wrong, but someone makes you feel that you have. Others may make you feel guilty or ashamed because *they themselves* feel inadequate. Such people have a habit of making themselves look better by making others look worse. Don't fall into that trap.

Unless you have committed a heinous crime against people, nature, or an innocent creature, you should not be living with large amounts of regret or guilt. You may have a few slips from time to time when you regret saying or doing something you wish you had not. But if you own up to it, make your apologies, and move on, you won't live your life swallowing bottles of self-pity, regret, or guilt—particularly with giant doses of grief and anger. Dwelling on regret and guilt is the wrong recipe for enjoying life.

> *Don't stumble over something behind you.*
> —Seneca, Roman philosopher[3]

FEARLESS FABULOUS FIVE

1.  Every time you find yourself looking back with regret, get out a piece of paper and write down what's bothering you and what, if anything, can be changed. If nothing can be changed, then write down five great things you *can* do to feel better. I also suggest writing down the five best things that have ever happened you and adding to that list as wonderful things occur. On days when you feel a cloud of regret approaching, pull out the list and read it to brighten your mood.

2.  I call this tip "from dwell to dwelling." Here's how it works: Every time I start feeling anxious or regretful, I tackle a room in my house and clean out some drawers, straighten a closet, or a rearrange a shelf. Cleaning out my house clears my head. While I am rearranging my dwelling, I use the time to rearrange my thoughts.

3.  Physical exercise is one of the best ways to reenergize your body and mind. Taking a class or walking with friends forces you to think about the present.

4.  If people around are dumping their pasts and their regrets onto your present, step away. You don't need to be a receptacle for their emotional garbage.

5.  It is perfectly natural to grieve for what you've lost or what you regret, but if grief is gobbling you up and rendering you incapable of functioning, you may want to seek professional counseling to get to the heart of the matter.

*A bend in the road is not the end of the road . . . unless you fail to make the turn.*
*—Helen Keller, American author*[4]

# SET YOUR PRIDE ASIDE

*It is better to lose your pride with someone you love rather than to lose that someone you love with your useless pride.*
*—Unknown*

**B**ouncing back after a setback is challenging. Comebacks and reinventions are all possible, but it can take a lot of soul-searching and time. Sometimes, you just have to set aside your pride and move forward.

A setback, whether personal, professional, or a combination of both, can put you into an emotional tailspin or even into emotional paralysis. Suddenly, you may feel like you're no longer in the driver's seat. Factors you cannot control are running and, in your mind, ruining your life.

A health setback has its own special course. You need to follow the directions of your authorities—in this case, your doctors—to become healthy again. Focus on your medical plan.

A financial setback, be it a disaster, debt, or the loss of your business or job, means you may have to adjust how you live and control your spending, or take on work you never wanted to do. Focus on staying afloat.

A personal setback, such as the breakup of a relationship or the death of a loved one, means you have to deal with profound loss; someone who used to be there for you emotionally and physically is gone. It's an emptiness like none other. Focus on filling that void.

With any of these setbacks, you may need to rely on people when you didn't before. You may need to adjust how you live and how you spend your time, money, or energies. Always, you'll need to adjust your attitude. It may take going a few steps backward or sideways to get back to moving forward.

Focus also on the process of healing. Setbacks are like steep switchbacks on a mountain trail. They can wear you down emotionally and physically before you complete the course. To heal your soul, you have to

35

first face your vulnerability and accept that you need time to heal and that you may need help. Many people are too proud to do this. They suffer in silence or sink into bitterness. Sometimes you need to set aside your pride.

But what does it really mean to set aside your pride? My diction-ary provided several definitions for *pride*. The first is "a sense of one's own . . . value; self-respect." The second is "pleasure or satisfaction taken in an achievement, possession, or association." The third is "a cause or a source of pleasure or satisfaction." And the fourth is "an excessively high opinion of oneself; conceit."[1]

Well, that's a wide set of definitions, ranging from "good pride" to "bad."

Don't ever lose your self-respect. And you should always have pride in what you accomplish, as well as in your beliefs. This is "good pride."

"Bad pride" is arrogance, an attitude that makes you inflexible or unrealistic. "I've always done it this way." "I am better than that." "I am too good to do that." "I refuse to change." That's the "bad pride" in the proverb, "Pride goeth before destruction, and an haughty spirit before a fall."[2]

So when I say you sometimes need to put aside your pride, I mean it this way: believe you can be yourself, and believe in yourself no matter what other people say. Know that sometimes circumstances may force you to adjust how you live and what you do. That is okay, provided it helps you move beyond your setback. Realize that the path you took to get where you are today may not be the best one for you to continue on to reach a better tomorrow. It may be better to jump off or take a detour. Who you are and what you are is your journey; don't expect others to walk your same path or keep up with you. Your journey may not be their choice of direction.

Setbacks mean that you will need to be more realistic. Don't compare yourself and your situation to anyone else, and don't criticize anyone else for being different. Swallow any arrogance you possess and and focus on the positive, as hard as that can be sometimes. Don't play the blame game. Instead, make a game plan.

Keep your good pride intact. Toss your bad pride aside.

*No one ever choked to death swallowing his pride.*
*—Unknown*

FEARLESS FABULOUS FIVE

1.  Never let your pride stand in the way of your progress.

2.  Being proud of your accomplishments is good pride, but being arrogant is bad pride.

3.  Humility is the realization that you don't ever have to be superhuman. It's perfectly fine to be yourself and not compete, contrast, or compare yourself with others.

4.  If you accept yourself with confidence, it will encourage others to do the same.

5.  Never make excuses or apologies for being true to yourself. Save apologies for when they really mean something and when they matter to those around you.

> *Pride is concerned with who is right.*
> *Humility is concerned with what is right.*
> —*Ezra Taft Benson, American author and former president of the Church of Jesus Christ of Latter-day Saints*[3]

# STEP OUTSIDE OF YOUR COMFORT ZONE

*The more you stay in your comfort zone, the smaller it gets. The more you leave your comfort, the bigger it gets.*
*—Unknown*

**A**re you still wearing the same hairstyle from college? Do you take the same route to work every day? Do you surround your-self with the same circle of friends? Do you eat the same foods or visit the same places? When was the last time you stepped off the curb of comfort into a lane of let's see what happens?

There is nothing wrong with the warmth of familiarity or maintaining your same sense of style and substance. Constancy can be comfortable, like the well-worn pajamas or bathrobe probably hanging in your closet. But sometimes you have to clean out your closet, discard what no longer fits, and try something new. Sameness can be translated into inflexibility or unwillingness to grow.

You can take things for granted when you get too comfortable or become complacent. This is especially true when dealing with people close to you or with certain living situations. Then something happens that reminds you that nothing actually stays the same, and what you thought was a constant may have only have been an extended moment in time. You might realize the only thing around that isn't changing is *you*. Perhaps you'll start to feel stuck or that life is passing you by.

If you're stuck in your comfort zone, maybe it's time to push the boundaries.

Some of my best *aha!* moments have come from stepping out of my comfort zone. It helps you gain perspective and see things—and also yourself—in a different light. I've always enjoyed the exhilaration of traveling alone to someplace where I know no one and may not even know the language. I love sitting alone in a restaurant, trying new foods, and picking up a conversation with random people sitting at a table next to me. My mind feels more alert, and my senses open up to the new sights, sounds, and smells around me.

I've stepped out of my comfort zone in other ways. I took a scuba diving class to explore the ocean and combat my claustrophobia. I've trekked in high mountains despite my fear of heights. I posed bare-breasted for a photographer working on an art exhibit featuring women who have had mastectomies to learn to feel comfortable again in my reconstructed body. I walked away from a large client with no financial safety net as a backup because no amount of money was worth the aggravation. Each experience reminded me that life is about possibility, not impossibility, if you open your mind and put doubt aside.

Stepping out of your comfort zone does not have to involve going to an extreme like quitting a job, breaking off a relationship, or selling your worldly possessions, but you may choose to do these things. It does not mean doing something that goes against your values, but you may do something totally out of character. It doesn't necessarily mean facing your fears, but it might. It may be as simple as trying something you have never done, changing an established routine, or walking into a room where you know absolutely no one and making an effort to meet people.

If you feel that your life is a bit crusty, stale, or dated, maybe it's time to pick off those pieces and have a taste of something new. Seasoning will add new flavor to a dull dish. Pruning dead leaves off a plant helps it grow. Start small and see what happens. It may lead to something more exhilarating and rewarding, or it may simply make you appreciate what you have even more. Either way, the experience of getting outside your comfort zone will help you grow. Stepping out of your comfort zone can feel like jumping off a ship sometimes, but a person with a buoyant spirit will manage to stay afloat.

> *A ship in port is safe. But that's not what ships are built for.*
> *Sail out to sea and do new things.*
> —*John Augustus Shedd, American author and professor*[1]

FEARLESS FABULOUS FIVE

1. Be the architect of your life. Expect to make renovations over time.

2. Build emotional bridges, not barriers. You are only confined by the walls you build around yourself.

3. Pushing the limits is healthy exercise for both your mind and your body. You will see better results by mixing up your routine.

4. Stepping out of your comfort zone is different than stepping into your panic zone. Learn to channel feelings of discomfort into the excitement of discovery.

5. Realize that stepping out of your comfort zone should be your choice, not someone else's decision for you. Nor should you expect others to jump in and join you.

> *If you obey all the rules, you miss all the fun.*
> —*Katherine Hepburn, American actress*[2]

**i. b.liev'n...** ®

"Finding My Passion!"

She said, as she Carefully Reached Way Down Deep Inside and Pulled to the Surface the One Thing that Brought her the Most Joy!

# Reconnect

**To thrive in life, you need three bones:**
**A wishbone**
**A backbone**
**And a funny bone**

—Reba McEntire, American country music artist
and actress

# TAKE STOCK OF YOUR TOOLBOX

*Everyone has a talent; it's just a matter of moving around*
*until you discover what it is.*
*—Georges Lucas American film director*[1]

**W**e **all have within us, in varying degrees, two power** tools that can help us build the life we envision: skillpower and willpower.

*Skillpower* is all the knowledge, skills, and other attributes that make you the essential *you*. It's the ability and talent that you can use and develop. Your tools, much like an artist's, are essential to your trade.

*Willpower* is your determination to make things happen. If you find you lack certain skills, your willpower will make sure you get the right training, information, or help to proceed.

Each person's toolbox is unique to them. My toolbox consists of my writing and speaking skills, creativity, business vision, connections, and knowledge of my industry. These are irreplaceable. Your toolbox has value. Don't take it for granted, and don't let others take advantage of it. How many times has someone said to you, "Can I pick your brain?" or, "Send me your ideas," or, "Will you share your list with me?" And how many times did it lead to anything other than the idea dustbin?

Don't give away the contents of your toolbox to people who don't give back, either in financial or emotional compensation. This is true whether you are finessing a business deal or entering into a new personal relationship. Don't let your toolbox become a Pandora's box that releases everything out and leaves you high and dry.

My late father always used to say, "Why buy the cow when the milk is free?" Now, what *he* was lecturing me on at the time was having sex before marriage. But his words ring true in other areas of life, especially when it comes to putting a value on who you are and what you have to offer. Don't give your generous heart away to someone who is not ready to accept and cherish it. Don't give your best ideas to people who should be paying for your intelligence. Don't give away the bar if people still owe you a tab. Don't let people take advantage of your time or talents unless you are consciously choosing to donate them.

Simply put: never sell yourself short. You are worth more than you think. Believe it.

Take some time to write down everything that you feel is an asset in your toolbox. Then, calculate how long it has taken you to develop and collect your assets. Use this information to decide how valuable each tool is to you. Add at least twenty percent more because you probably are undervaluing yourself. If you set your price too low, you'll just have to climb higher to make it where you want to be. Remember, for everything you do, there is "the cost of doing business," which I also call "the aggravation factor."

Make a list of the things that no longer belong in your toolbox—what is cluttering it up? These are your liabilities. Then calculate what it will take to eliminate them so that your toolbox is lighter and more open to new skills and ideas. For example, I realized that managing my business accounting was not my best skill and was an inefficient use of my time. I invested in a reliable and patient bookkeeper to keep things in order. This freed up my time to work on developing new business. I lack certain technical skills and patience with my website and blog. I work with a technical wizard who can make necessary updates and design changes faster and better than I can. This enables me to focus on writing content, which is something I enjoy and do well.

Your toolbox needs to be cleaned out and reassessed every so often. Just like your makeup drawer, which is probably filled with old lipsticks, eye shadows, and blushes that are no longer usable, your toolbox needs to be cleaned out every so often and refreshed. It can become obsolete if it's not cared for properly. I finally threw out my typewriter when I moved offices. It had been sitting on a desk unused and taking up space for years.

Your toolbox should never become an emotional junk box. Your toolbox is about building and maintaining skills to help you grow and thrive, not hoarding regrets or disappointments. Find another outlet to release your anxieties, and keep your toolbox productive. When I am feeling stressed at the end of the workday, I may take a walk outside, play with my dog, take a refreshing shower to cool off my hot emotions, or express myself by writing in my diary. When your thoughts start to jumble, try to detach from what you are doing, even for a short time, and create mental and physical space to clear your head. Keep your toolbox from negative mental debris.

Your toolbox is your treasure chest. Your skills and talents and education are your present and future to utilize to pursue your dreams if you choose. Treasure them, because no one can take away knowledge once you have acquired it.

> *Use what talent you possess: the woods would be very silent*
> *if no birds sang except those that sang best.*
> —*Henry van Dyke, American clergyman, educator, author*[2]

## FEARLESS FABULOUS FIVE

1. Build your toolbox with skills you enjoy, that make you unique, and, above all, boost your self-worth.

2. Your skills and talents are unique to you. You don't have to match them up to anyone else's if you enjoy them and they work for you. Avoid comparing or taking on something that doesn't fit your personality.

3. Every so often, it is important to take stock by getting rid of anything that is not going to take you forward.

4. Be open to adding new tools and skills. Learning keeps your mind vibrant and your professional marketability relevant.

5. Share your skills as a mentor to cultivate someone else. And let that person share with you. It's amazing what you can learn by sharing.

> *We are always more anxious to be distinguished for a talent which we do not*
> *possess, than for the fifteen which we do possess.*
> —*Mark Twain*[3]

# FIND YOUR VOICE

*Don't let the noise of others' opinions drown out your own inner voice.*
—*Steve Jobs, CEO and cofounder of Apple and Pixar*[1]

**I think we all have a voice inside of us that embodies our** personal and creative expression. Some of us have several voices. The key is finding your voice and using it.

My voice is in my writing. The written word enables me to express myself in ways I cannot speak aloud. If I lost the gift of gab forever, I know I would be able to share my ideas and creativity through my writing.

Artists find their voices in myriad ways, from paint to pen to pencil to performance. Dancers express themselves through movement. Cooks put a dose of expression in the foods they prepare. Writers coin words. Photographers take pictures. Activists rally others to speak out. Some people show their voice by their actions: giving time or sharing expertise. Others share their voice quietly, through small gestures and soft words.

Creativity is not always required to find your voice, but ingenuity is. Too often, our lives are so cluttered by information and chores and listening to others that we forget to take the time to express ourselves. We say to ourselves, "I don't have the time."

But you do have your unique gift of expression, and you can make time for it if you choose. You should never make petty excuses to hide your voice behind being too busy or fearful. The opportunity may pass you by. Creative expression should not be suppressed. How would we ever experience the beauty of a painting or a song if people were too busy to take the time to create them?

There is a book called *The Diving Bell and the Butterfly* by French journalist Jean-Dominique Bauby. Bauby suffered a massive stroke that resulted in a rare condition called "locked-in syndrome." He was physically paralyzed with the exception of some movement in his head and his left eye. To most, he was left unable to communicate. But by blinking his one good eye and working with a transcriber, this man dictated his book over the course of ten months and an estimated 200,000 blinks. *The Diving Bell and the Butterfly* became a bestseller in Europe and was later made into a movie. Imagine what would have happened if Bauby remained locked in his thoughts.

Citizens around the world have fought hard for the right to have freedom of speech, usually paying a heavy price in human lives. But freedom of speech does not always translate into the ability to communicate. That's why there are numerous practitioners and books that teach communications skills. And even still, many people remain afraid to express their voice for fear of criticism. How can citizens who fight for freedom of speech turn and silence each other's voices with threats or derision? Instead, you should focus on words and acts that encourage expression.

Expression is a powerful thing. Great orators have moved masses. Yet the soft voice of a mother telling a story to her child is just as powerful. You should listen to your inner voice first to make sure that what you say out loud and how you express yourself is productive and not hurtful. You can always change the tone of your voice, but you can never retract words or actions. Use your expression for the purpose of good. If you've found your voice, you're a lucky person. If you're still searching, what's holding you back?

*If you hear a voice within you say "you can't paint," then by all means, paint,*
*and that voice will be silenced.*
*—Vincent van Gogh, Dutch artist*[2]

FEARLESS FABULOUS FIVE

1. Everybody has a creative voice tucked inside them. Sometimes it just needs to be coaxed out.

2. The best ways to unlock your voice is through a creative outlet and an open mind.

3. Never let stress or petty day-to-day annoyances put you in expressive lockdown.

4. If you need help, take a class, join a group, or simply try something new to bring out your personal expression.

5. Do not let someone silence *your* voice because they are not willing to listen.

> *Life is not about finding yourself. Life is about creating yourself.*
> —*George Bernard Shaw, Irish playwright, socialist, and a cofounder of the London School of Economics*[3]

# TURN ROADBLOCKS INTO BUILDING BLOCKS

*"For every failure, there's an alternative course of action.
You just have to find it. When you come to a roadblock, take a detour."*
—Mary Kay Ash, Founder of Mary Kay Inc.[1]

**D**uring my years as a professional event planner, I learned that even with the best planning, things can go awry. You plan for something to go wrong inasmuch as you plan for everything to go right. Two examples:

In 2005, Hurricane Katrina caused massive destruction to my beloved city of New Orleans. My company was in the middle of planning a major destination weekend event in the city, and almost everyone we were working with in New Orleans had evacuated and, in most cases, was unreachable. We assessed the situation and did our best to keep planning what we could. Eventually, we realized the event would need to be cancelled—the roadblock was too much to fix at that time. However, several months later, we produced a tribute to the culinary heritage of New Orleans at the 2006 James Beard Foundation Awards. It was a beautiful evening recognizing the historical and cultural significance of this great city and the strength of those who withstood the hurricane. We turned a roadblock into a building block. In this case, we helped promote rebuilding New Orleans.

A nice side story to the tribute was that my then-boyfriend, David Ransom, came onstage to propose marriage in front of two thousand attendees. We decided to plan a destination wedding in New Orleans on March 17, 2007—St. Patrick's Day. But there was no luck that day for us. A nor'easter cancelled all flights out of New York, and many of our close friends were unable to make it to New Orleans to attend our wedding. I didn't panic or dwell on my disappointment. With a phone call to a friend in the restaurant business, I booked a location in New York to stage a wedding reenactment for all our friends on the Wednesday after our wedding. Everyone was told to "dress for a ceremony." I wore my wedding gown again and showed the video of the actual ceremony in New Orleans on a large screen. Everyone was happy and grateful that we went the extra mile. We transformed a roadblock into a building block for our friendships. All it took was ingenuity and the right attitude.

Of course, roadblocks are relative to the individual and the situation. My wedding weather drama is a pittance of a problem when compared to those who lost loved ones in the World Trade Center attacks, the Boston Marathon bombing, or any other number of catastrophes. You cannot compare apples to oranges.

But what you can draw from all survivor stories, large and small, is the inspiration to come back with a strong attitude and determination not to let your roadblock derail your life. You may need to make physical, emotional, and economic adjustments, but you can rearrange your roadblocks to make your foundation strong.

Everyone faces a roadblock at some point in life. The keys to navigating around or jumping over the hurdle are your confidence in yourself, your faith (whether emotional or spiritual), your determination, your wit, your smarts, and your sense of humor. And a great support team to help you recover will help immeasurably as well.

All is not lost unless you lose all hope. Even the worst-case scenario can teach you a lesson. And if a door is slammed in your face, start knocking elsewhere. Do not give in or give up unless you've decided on a better option—or choose to settle on your terms. As an unknown author once said and many have repeated, "The only difference between stumbling blocks and stepping stones is how you use them."

> *Doubts in your mind are a much greater roadblock to success than obstacles on the journey.*
> —*Orrin Woodward and Chris Brady,*
> *Authors and cofounders of LIFE Leadership*[2]

## FEARLESS FABULOUS FIVE

1. If you hit a roadblock, analyze it to determine what is causing it and whether it can be moved or changed. Is it a roadblock you created for yourself, or did someone or something set it up against

you? If it simply cannot be changed—as is the case with physical limitations and circumstances beyond your control—then weigh your options, choose the best one, and focus on it.

2.  If you're facing an emotional roadblock, it's important to understand and work through the factors that created it so that you can better understand how to navigate around it. Professional coaching or counseling may help.

3.  You may need to change your direction or your goals if you keep facing the same roadblocks without making progress. Don't keep knocking your head against a wall!

4.  Something that may appear to be a roadblock may actually be nothing more than a major inconvenience and not an obstacle. Decide how much it really matters to you and whether want to go in another direction. The wrong attitude can be your biggest obstacle.

5.  Major roadblocks, such as illness, death, disability, or natural disasters, will take more time to overcome. Patience, fortitude, confidence, faith, determination, and wit will help guide you, along with a great support network. This is a time to lean on your support network to be lifted up.

*When something bad happens you can have three choices. You can either let it define you, let it destroy you, or you can let it strengthen you.*
*—Unknown*

# ALLOW SERENDIPITY TO ALIGHT ON YOUR SHOULDER

*Life is what happens to us while we are making other plans.*
*—Allen Saunders, American author and cartoonist*[1]

I have always been an overachiever—a planner with a to-do list, a timeline, and a goal.

My husband, on the other hand, lives life rather serendipitously. He's a man with no plan, yet amazing opportunities casually come his way and he calmly accepts them. No wonder he never looks stressed!

A good friend once told me, "Maybe you should stop trying so hard. Just let things fall where they may and see what transpires." It was good advice, and I try to follow it. When I do, I feel much calmer. Allowing for a little serendipity in my life led to a feeling of serenity. I learned that when I stopped striving to make things happen, I found more time to enjoy what was already happening around me. In the process, more doors seemed to open to new opportunities—or perhaps my mind opened up to more possibilities.

*Serendipity* by definition means "finding valuable or agreeable things not sought for"[2]—a pleasant surprise. In other words, you cannot seek serendipity. It alights upon you, often when you least expect it. It's a gift.

I think serendipity brought my husband, David, and me together. Flashback to a 2003 dinner party given by my dear friend Sophia from London, who also was an ex-girlfriend of David's many years earlier. Dozens of friends and acquaintances gathered at a small Italian restaurant below ground zero in lower Manhattan that a few of us "adopted" after the terrorist attacks to support downtown businesses. When I walked in, David was the first person I saw. I didn't recognize him at first; it had been a long time since we had seen each other. We connected instantly and exchanged numbers. It was strange. If September 11th had not occurred, would we have adopted Giovanni's Atrium? Would David have been in the process of relocating back to New York? Would Sophia have flown to New York from London to visit friends and host the dinner party? Would our lives be different today? Unexpected good things can grow out of even the most horrific events.

Being a devout over-planner, goal-setter, and list-maker all of my life are habits that have served me well in my business. They keep me focused and in charge, and they have made me a successful event planner. But the best lesson I ever learned to reduce anxiety was to sit back and let things fall where they may. The laws of nature have their own rules, and they can't be systemized to fit into your life. You have to adapt to nature. Things happen that are not in your control. What you can control is how you face them.

I love this quote by inspirational author and artist Vivian Greene: "Life is not about waiting for the storm to pass. . . . It is about learning to dance in the rain."[3] This quote is displayed on a piece of art over my front door to remind me every time I step outside that it's up to me to determine my outlook. Sometimes you just have kick up your feet and say, "Come what may, everything is going to work out." The best way to experience serendipity is by living your life and pursuing what you enjoy, what you believe in, and what you can share with others. I truly believe that by doing this, serendipity will find you.

And when it does, you will be truly blessed.

*Life is a series of natural and spontaneous changes. Don't resist them; that only creates sorrow. Let reality be reality. Let things flow naturally forward in whatever way they like.*
*—Unknown*

FEARLESS & FABULOUS FIVE

1. Serendipity, like happiness, is priceless. It cannot be bought or sold, but the expression can be easily shared.

2. Smiles tend to attract serendipity. So do open minds and hearts.

3. Serendipity grows on sincerity. If the song in your heart rings false, serendipity likely won't follow you.

4. Sometimes you can reach for too much. Unlock your grip and lighten up.

5.  Anticipation is one thing; expectation is another. Don't set yourself up for disappointment by demanding too much of yourself or others.

*Serendipity: Look for something, find something else and realize that what you've found is more suited to your needs than what you were looking for.*
*—Lawrence Block, American mystery and crime novelist*[A]

# A Poem of Gratitude

I first heard this poem when I was age five, and it made a lasting impression To this day I repeat it when I need to re-center myself.

## The World Is Mine

*Today on a bus, I saw a lovely girl with silken hair*
*I envied her; she seemed so gay, and I wished I was so fair.*
*When suddenly she rose to leave, I saw her hobble down the aisle.*
*She had one leg and bore a crutch, but as she passed a smile*
*O' God forgive me when I whine.*
*I have two legs; the world is mine.*
*And then I stopped to buy some sweets.*
*The lad who served me had such charm.*
*I talked with him; he seemed so calm, and if I were late it would do no harm.*
*And as I left he said to me, "I thank you, you have been so kind."*
*"It's nice to talk with folks like you. You see, I'm blind."*
*O' God forgive me when I whine.*
*I have two eyes, the world is mine.*
*Later walking down the street, I saw a child with eyes of blue.*
*He stood and watched the others play; it seemed he knew not what to do.*
*I stopped a moment, then I said, "why don't you join the others dear?"*
*He looked ahead without a word, and then I knew he could not hear."*
*O' God forgive me when I whine*
*I have two ears, the world is mine.*
*With legs to take me where I'll go*
*With eyes to see the sunset's glow*
*With ears to hear what I would know*
*O' God forgive me when I whine*
*I'm blessed indeed, the world is mine*

*—Author Unknown*

# FILL YOUR ATTITUDE WITH GRATITUDE

*Gratitude teaches us to appreciate the rainbow and the storm.*
—*Dr. Christina G. Hibbert, American clinical psychologist and author*[1]

**hy is it that some individuals who seem to have it all** complain so frequently about being overwhelmed? Isn't having it all what we all wanted when we first started out in life? And why do other people who appear to have so little and struggle so hard to stay afloat express gratitude for what they have?

It's all in the attitude. And gratitude is the best attitude.

The day I stopped fixating on what I had not achieved in my life and started being grateful for all that I had was the day I became a more centered and calm person. When I stopped comparing what I had or did not have to others, I became a happier person. It wasn't about being complacent; it was about being appreciative.

Learning to practice gratitude will not only make you a happier person, it will make you a more attractive person to others. Gratitude makes you glow. It shows your inner beauty.

Gratitude makes other people feel better. Making other people feel better about themselves will reflect back on you. Everyone wants to be around people who make them feel good. Think about friends whose companionship you enjoy most. They make you laugh. They are kind and considerate of you. They let you know how much they appreciate you. People who express gratitude tend to be less critical and more compassionate, and that makes them more pleasant to be around.

Life coaches will tell you to count ten reasons to be grateful every day. It helps put you in mental check. But counting ten reasons for you to be grateful about your life is still looking inward. You can lie in bed and stare at your navel and think about all the reasons to be grateful in your life, or you can get up and be proactive about it.

How about looking outward and expressing your gratitude? Write a thank-you note to those individuals who have helped you along the way. Call a friend—don't text or email—to say hello and brighten his or her day. Bring food to someone who's under the weather or offer to run errands. Deliver more compliments and less criticism. Let someone know how much you appreciate all he or she does. Expressing your appreciation to someone may be just the gift that person needs at that time. Never be afraid to say "thank you" or "great job" or "I'm happy you're here." It's amazing how many people don't do this enough and then, when it's too late, regret not saying it.

You will be a happier person if you expend more energy on being grateful for what you have rather than wishful for what you do not have. Most of us are so busy planning our next steps that we don't allow ourselves the time to sit back and enjoy what we have in front of us.

I learned about giving and expressing gratitude by working in a business centered on hospitality. Offering a warm welcome and a positive experience to someone who may have had a hard day at work or a long journey to reach you is equally gratifying for both the person who gives and the person who receives. It expends the same energy to hand out smiles instead of frowns, and compliments rather than complaints. Yet the positive action feels so much more energizing than the negative one does.

Even though *gratitude* is a noun, it is expressed by actions. Start by complimenting more and criticizing less. Acts of gratitude are even stronger than words. Sharing your gratitude with others will bring double happiness, both to the person you are thanking and to yourself. Gratitude is a great gift to pass on. Don't let moments of feeling grateful and expressing your gratitude pass you by because you're too wrapped up in other things. Instead, wrap your head around being thankful for what you have, for how hard you worked for it, and for those who supported you along the way.

> *Feeling gratitude and not expressing it is like*
> *wrapping a present and not giving it.*
> *—William Arthur Ward, American author*[2]

FEARLESS FABULOUS FIVE

1.  Every day, make a mental list of five things you are grateful for. If you can get to ten, even better.

2.  Once a week, write or call someone who has been there for you and say thank you. You never know how much it means or how much it can brighten someone's day.

3.  Acknowledge the people who help you in stores, banks, nail salons, restaurants, and so on by name (they may well be wearing a name tag). Talk *to* them instead of *at* them.

4.  Share your gratitude by giving your time, talents, or other resources to help someone else. "Paying it forward" is one of the best ways to expand your gratitude.

5.  If someone pays you a compliment or congratulates you for an achievement, don't respond with an excuse or say, "It was nothing." Simply say, "Thank you. I appreciate it," or, "You are welcome." Expressing gratitude does not need justification. Being gracious is simply enough.

*Piglet noticed that even though he had a very small heart, it could hold a rather large amount of gratitude.*
*—A.A. Milne, Author of* Winnie-the-Pooh[3]

i. b.liev'n...®

"a Light that Always Shines with a Little Change in my Perspective!"

She said, Realizing that Sometimes All it Took was Putting a New Frame Around an Old Situation to Create a New Opportunity!

# Reframe

"My dear fellow, who will let you?"
"That's not the point. The point is, who
will stop me?"

—Ayn Rand, *The Fountainhead*

# REFRAME FOR A NEW PERSPECTIVE

*She stood in the storm, and when the wind did not*
*blow her way . . . she adjusted her sails.*
—Elizabeth Edwards, American author[1]

**A** faceless snowman opened his Christmas gift and felt two lumps of coal.

"What?! You are giving me two lumps of coal?" he exclaimed with disappointment to the giver.

"Let me show you how to use them," responded the giver. And she placed the lumps of coal on the snowman's empty face.

"Wow! Now I can see!" said the snowman.

"You did not need lumps of coal to see," said the giver. "Vision comes from within."

I was inspired to write this from an illustration on a Christmas card of a child placing lumps of coal on a snowman to create eyes. At the time, I was working to reenvision my life after feeling like a large pile of coal had been dumped on me. I thought about the coal as a metaphor for how you can reframe your view of life and fuel your imagination.

The term "lumps of coal" is usually referred to as a negative—a bad gift. But in reality, here's the coal, hard truth: Lumps of coal can represent seeds of vision. It is all about perspective. The Chinese view coal as dirty and bad. The Scottish give lumps coal of as good luck gifts on New Year's Day. You burn coal to create warmth; you can cook with charcoal to create a meal to nourish loved ones. Some view burning coal as dirty, polluting. Yet charcoal is used to filter and purify water. Charcoal can be used to create beautiful works of art to be displayed—or create dirty smudges to be cleaned. You can view coal as fuel to fire up new ideas.

Like diamonds, coal is made of carbon—as are we. All three are born rough, yet with care and vision, the diamond becomes a thing of beauty, coal becomes the heat that warms our homes, and we can become whatever we desire.

Take the lumps of coal life tosses your way and use them not just to create warmth but also to fire up new ideas and create something special. It's all how you view it.

But you must keep both your mind and eyes open to possibility. Do you have a blind spot that is impacting your vision? Lack of vision and fear of facing a situation with your eyes and mind open are reasons we fail to move forward. And all the money in the world will get you nowhere if you don't know where you want to go or believe you can't get there. Keep your eye on a goal or a direction to propel you forward. I had a friend who had serious eye surgery in both eyes. She tried to stay upbeat, but with a fearful tone in her voice, she told me, "I'm so afraid I will lose my eyesight."

I told her, "You will not lose your eyesight. Don't be afraid. You will come out of this with more clarity and a clearer vision of what really matters."

When I faced chemotherapy treatment and dreaded the idea of being infused by what I believed were poisonous drugs, a dear friend and fellow cancer survivor told me, "Don't think of poison entering your body; think of your system being cleansed from toxic cancer." That advice taught me the essence of reframing. I looked at those five months as a means of getting healthy, not as a time of becoming sick. To this day, I try and reframe every negative situation into something as positive and healthy as I can make it.

As a communications specialist, I was trained in facing challenges and spinning stories to reframe negative outcomes for my clients. Learning to do it in my own life was an entirely different experience. It starts with having a clear view of who you are, how you look at things, and how you want to be perceived. How you envision yourself and who you want to be should be the fuel that keeps you going. Refusing to look at things with fresh perspective will only hold you back.

Reframing is physical as well as mental. Much in the same way you can reframe a painting to give a fresh new look, you can change your wardrobe, the interior of your home, your looks, or where you live to have a fresh, new perspective. I moved from a large city to a small country town where I felt it was more conducive to write and relax. However, if you make a physical change, make sure it's to open your mind, not to cover up your problems.

The next time you feel life has dumped a pile of coal on you, remember, that black stuff in the bin could become artwork, fuel, or even diamonds if you clear the dust from your eyes. Reframe and you'll see possibilities.

*No one ever injured their eyesight by looking on the bright side of things.*
*—Unknown*

FEARLESS FABULOUS FIVE

1. If you no longer like the picture of your life, maybe it's time to reframe it.

2. Where one person sees lumps of useless coal, another sees fuel to stay warm. Perception can take you down a positive or negative path.

3. Know that not everyone will see eye-to-eye with you. Keep the vision of the life you want clear, and don't let others' opinions cloud your view.

4. When something bad happens to you or a loved one, reframing your perspective will be hard. It will take time. But it will make you stronger, and it will make your mental vision clearer.

5. If you reframe the situation and still don't like what you see, try again. If it still doesn't work for you, maybe it's time to change the picture and not just the frame.

*The way we choose to see the world creates the world we see.*
*—Barry Neil Kaufman, Cofounder and*
*codirector of the Option Institute[2]*

# DEFINE SUCCESS YOUR WAY

*Success is a journey . . . not a destination.*
—*Unknown*

**W**hat is your vision of success? Is it in clear sight or in hindsight? Or neither?

When I meet with prospective clients, I ask them, "What is your vision of success if we work together?" Many cannot answer this question because they haven't defined what success means to them. Sometimes it's a quantifiable objective, like more sales and increased profit. Other times it is a qualitative goal, such as "being recognized as a leader in my field" or "being a good and providing parent."

Success, much like happiness and peace of mind, is something you need to define on your own terms. One person's version of success may not be yours, and you should never allow anyone to size you up by their terms. Over time your definition of success may change, which is healthy.

When I was a very young girl, I felt making straight As on my report card was a success. Academia and accolades are important in my family, and I was encouraged to excel in everything I pursued. As a teenager, being popular in school with lots of friends and voted into the dance troupe was my idea of success. I wanted to fit in. Then I took a job freelance writing for the local newspaper, and my idea of success changed. I wanted to grow up and become a successful and famous magazine editor-in-chief. I wanted to stand out.

I was voted "Most Likely to Succeed" in high school. At the time, it was a huge honor. I felt it validated who I was and where I was heading in my life. But over time, the honor felt more like a burden—something I had to live up to, and not necessarily by my own standards.

No one gave me a road map to go with the title; I had to find my way and define what "success" really meant to me. As an adult, my definition of "success" meant having a successful career, a happy marriage, and the freedom and means to travel. These are still important to me. But I now define success as living with purpose, joy, and contentment—without regrets or fear. For some, *success* is tied to money, power, and prestige. Businesses define success by their profits. Athletes succeed by winning. Still others consider success to be achieving something they have always wanted to do or making a difference for others.

The words *success* and *achievement* are often used interchangeably. Among *Merriam-Webster*'s definitions of *success* include 1) the fact of getting or achieving wealth, respect, or fame, 2) a favorable or desirable outcome, and 3) one that succeeds.[1] In contrast, the dictionary's definitions of *achievement* are 1) the act of achieving: accomplishment, 2a) a result gained by effort, 2b) a great or heroic deed, and 3) the quality and quantity of a student's work.[2] Wouldn't it be better to define who we are by our specific achievements and efforts rather than others' definitions of success?

A business colleague who worked as a Senior Brand Director at a wine marketing company once said to me, "Maybe if you'd earned an MBA, you would be more successful." Given that I'd run a successful business for twenty years and he was still advancing up the senior rungs on the corporate ladder of a large company, I thought it was a strange comment. I replied, "Your definition of success is clearly different than mine."

Over the years, as I checked off the rungs on my achievement ladder, I started feeling confined by my own definition of success. Despite all my achievements, I constantly felt pressured to be more successful, and I was always worried about losing business. I had invested heavily in time and money to grow my business and become recognized as outstanding in my field. But the demands to stay competitive and relevant in a shifting industry and economy were impacting my well-being. The bar I had set was starting to weigh me down, and the price I was paying was too costly to my physical and emotional health. I wanted freedom from my pressure to compete and my fear of failure.

I wanted to redefine my vision of success as a process to define how I wanted to live. As an exercise, I sat down and wrote my obituary (try it!). Reading it over, I saw an impressive list of career accomplishments and travel escapades, and that was it. I decided "successful food and beverage public relations executive who enjoyed world traveling" was not how I wanted my legacy to read. The next chapters of my life needed to be rewritten with new material.

I realized that building bridges was more important to me than climbing ladders. Having a strong, balanced personal foundation meant

more to me than having it all. And inspiring others was even more important than earning accolades for myself. My priority went from focusing
on my *aspirations* to doing more to be an *inspiration* to make what I do
more impactful.

I learned to appreciate the positive impact of my accomplishments
and worry less about what I had not achieved and any negative feelings of
inadequacy. I also learned to stop evaluating others by what they had or
had not achieved, and I stopped expecting more from those whose mea-
surement of success did not match up with mine. By managing my own
expectations, it became easier to appreciate what others offered.

If I went back to the high school that honored me with the accolade
"Most Likely to Succeed," I would ask them to replace the title with "Most
Likely to Make a Difference." And I would tell the girls, "When you look
at your own definition of success, view it on what *your* hopes and dreams
are and not what others expect of you. Success is not a pass-fail grade,
and how you evaluate the sum of your success and why it matters is your
decision."

> *My mother drew a distinction between achievement and success. She said
> that achievement is the knowledge that you have studied and worked hard
> and done the best that is in you. Success is being praised by others, and that's
> nice too, but not as important or satisfying. Always aim for
> achievement and forget about success.*
> —Helen Hayes, American actress[3]

## FEARLESS FABULOUS FIVE

1.  Success should not be a pass-fail grade to assess our lives and who
    we are. One can be successful in many ways, and everyone can be
    successful at something.

2.  Achievement is a measure of who we are and how we make an
    impact. Success is a measure of what we accomplish.

3.  The price of being successful may not always be worth the cost
    of achieving it. If you do not have time to enjoy your success
    because you are always working to maintain it, or if negatively
    impacts your physical, emotional, or financial health, then you
    might want to rethink what success means to you.

4.  It is not necessary to be successful at everything you do. Just do

the best you can and be proud of it. It is perfectly okay to be perfectly imperfect.

5. Success is not about pleasing everyone else. It is about deriving pleasure from what you are doing, not what others want you to do.

> *Work for a cause, not for applause.*
> *Live life to express, not to impress*
> *Don't strive to make your presence noticed,*
> *just make your absence felt.*
> *—Unknown*

## FAMOUS FAILURES . . . WHO LATER SUCCEEDED[4]

*Not every wildly successful person started out on the right road. Here are some:*

1. Nobel Prize Award winning physicist Albert Einstein was expelled from high school for being a poor student.

2. Author J. K. Rowling was a single mother on welfare until her *Harry Potter* books made her a billionaire.

3. Film director Steven Spielberg was rejected from three film schools before one accepted him. He later dropped out, and then went on to make some of the most famous films of the century.

4. Basketball great Michael Jordan was cut from his high school basketball team.

5. Walt Disney was fired by a newspaper editor because he "lacked imagination and had no good ideas."

6. Harvard College dropout Bill Gates started a business called Traf-O-Data with Paul Allen. It floundered. They later co-founded Microsoft.

7. R. H. Macy had seven failed businesses before starting his renowned department store.

8. Nobel Prize–winning British prime minister Winston Churchill failed the sixth grade. He was defeated in numerous elections for public office until he became prime minister at the age of sixty-two.

9. Early in her career, Oprah Winfrey was fired from a job as a television reporter because she was "unfit for television."

# HAPPINESS IS WITHIN REACH. OPEN YOUR MIND

*Plenty of people miss their share of happiness, not because they never found it,*
*but because they didn't stop to enjoy it.*
*—William Feather, American author*[1]

**hat makes you happy? And is it within reach?**
Who is the happier person—the ambitious person who reaches higher and higher but remains restless, or the placid person who reaches out and not up, embraces what's close and seeks nothing more?

Which one are you? Or are you a combination?

My dad always told me to aim high and be a success. And I did it in a short amount of time. At twenty-two, I was working on glamorous travel and leisure accounts for a public relations firm in Atlanta. I won an industry award for a radio station account. At twenty-five, I moved to New York to work for a large agency and won another industry accolade for a frozen yogurt client. At thirty, I launched my first company and helped create many high profile food and beverage industry programs. By age forty, I was the focus of a television segment called "Who's Making It in New York." I never rested, not even on my laurels. I was always restless, aiming higher, trying to do more. I was fiercely competitive and constantly comparing myself to others. But then the sky fell: The economy collapsed. The business environment changed. I was diagnosed with cancer. My father died. It was beyond stressful. The experience made me refocus and reassess my concept of happiness.

Happiness is not how far you go or how high you fly but how centered and content you are within. Stop focusing so much on what you do not have or what you have not accomplished and start appreciating more what you do have and what you have achieved. Happiness is not a place, a region, a city, or a state. It is a state of mind. You can travel and be happy, but you cannot travel to find happiness. It is also immaterial. You can purchase something that makes you happy, but you cannot buy happiness. Happiness is only elusive to those who keep their eyes and minds closed to the possibility of *being* happy.

I think the people who are happiest may simply have more manageable expectations on what they expect from themselves or from other people. They live in a state of mental satisfaction versus emotional suspension. They spend more time being active and involved with their community, colleagues, or friends rather than isolated or dwelling on what could or should be. They have expectations in life, but maybe they just don't expect too much or dwell on the downside if things don't happen as planned.

People with lower expectations do not necessarily have lower standards about what they believe in or expect of themselves or others. They appreciate quality and especially quality of life. Their standards of measuring what quality means may be different and perfectly fine for them. People with high expectations don't always have the best standards of quality. Some are never happy because nothing is ever good enough.

Your vision of happiness can become clearer when you refocus your gaze. You don't have to don a pair of rose-colored glasses to have a better view of what matters—all you need is a brighter outlook and some insight. You really don't need to achieve a thing to be truly happy, and life does not owe you anything. Life simply leases you some time on Earth to do what you want with it. You hold the keys that can free your mind, open your heart, and unlock your happiness . . . or not.

Happiness was always within my reach—I was just grasping at the wrong things. Take the time to look around yourself and appreciate what's within your reach.

> *People take different roads seeking fulfillment and happiness. Just because they're not on your road doesn't mean they've gotten lost.*
> —*His Holiness The Dalai Lama XIV*[2]

FEARLESS FABULOUS FIVE

1.  Happiness is not cookie cutter; what makes you happy might not work for others. Be your own barometer for happiness. Don't measure your life against anyone else's.

2.  Happiness is what you do with your life, not what you do for a living. Happiness is not about how much money you make but about how you make the money work to improve your life and the lives of others.

3.  Happiness does not have a price tag. It can be neither bought nor sold. It is an intangible joy that's free to anyone. A poor woman filled with joy is better than a wealthy one filled with misery.

4.  Happiness is looking around you and enjoying what you have and not focusing on what you do not have.

5.  The best way to increase your happiness is to share it with others.

*The happiest people don't necessarily have the best of everything; they just make the best of everything they have.*
*—Unknown*

# EXPAND HORIZONS, BUT
# SET BOUNDARIES

*The real voyage of discovery consists not in seeking new landscapes,*
*but in having new eyes.*
—*Marcel Proust, French novelist[1]*

**I grew up in the small southern city of Chattanooga, Ten-**nessee. As a teenager, I longed to expand my horizons beyond the South and explore the world. I spent more than twenty years traveling for work and play, living in various cities, socializing with people of different cultures, and tasting the banquet that life has to offer—with second helpings. It has been the best education I could have. It has taught me acceptance, tolerance, and the ability to think outside the box. It has also taught me to appreciate the little town where I was born, which has since grown up to become a thriving city. Like Dorothy in the Land of Oz, I always wanted leave Kansas and roam the world. The more I traveled, the more I came to realize that there really was no place like home. But I had to set out on my journey to gain this perspective. Sometimes you need to spread your branches to better appreciate your roots.

You don't have to go on long journeys to faraway places to expand your horizons. You simply need to open your mind and be willing to learn new things, acquire new skills, and meet new people. Adventure is a short step away if you have a healthy imagination. You can open the pages of a book and dive into another country, try new cuisines at a nearby restaurant or from a cookbook, and watch great performances on the computer. The Internet has enabled us to expand our horizons and our minds in a multitude of ways. These days you do not always have to be on the go to go far and have great experiences.

But you can go too far, and that's where setting boundaries becomes important. Reaching too far, too high, and too fast without boundaries can backfire. You have to set boundaries to define who you are and what you will tolerate so that others will not take advantage of you. You have to set boundaries to maintain your well-being. At the same time, recognize the boundaries that others may establish when they feel pressured or fearful. There are boundaries that keep you healthy and your relationships strong, and there are walls that confine you and close everything in. Know the difference.

Boundaries can be lines of defense or offense. Understand when you can push them and when you should walk away. You can usually change your direction or change your mind. You may not always be able to change a situation—just how you deal with it.

But remember, with every boundary you set or face, there is also a horizon ahead.

> *Twenty years from now you will be more disappointed by the things you didn't do than by the ones you did do. So throw off the bowlines. Sail away from the safe harbor. Catch the trade winds in your sails.*
> *Explore. Dream. Discover.*
> —H. Jackson Brown Jr., American author[2]

## FEARLESS FABULOUS FIVE

1. Opening your mind is taking the first step toward expanding your horizons. An open wallet may finance an adventure, but if you are going with a closed mind, why bother?

2. In order to grow, you need to push your limits and stretch your imagination. Take a chance; be curious.

3. Education is an important way to expand horizons; hands-on experience and exploring will take you even further.

4. Learn to walk the line between setting boundaries and pushing them. Be diplomatic, not condescending, when dealing with people.

5. Make sure the boundaries you set and horizons you seek are your choices and are not forced on you.

> *Shoot for the moon. Even if you miss, you will land among the stars.*
> —Les Brown, American author and motivational speaker[3]

# EMBRACE YOUR
# AUTHENTICITY

*Always be a first-rate version of yourself instead of
a second-rate version of someone else.*
—Judy Garland, American actress and singer[1]

**L**ife's kind of funny when it comes to flip-flopping. As a teenager, you take great pains to fit in and be one of the gang. No one wants to be the odd person out. But as you grow older, you work harder to stand out and be noticed when competing for a job, pitching a new idea, or attracting someone to you.

I remember crying tears of self-pity when the general manager at a public relations agency in Atlanta where I worked told me to tone down my stylish attire and outspoken personality. I had just been turned down for a promotion to move to New York to work for our agency's parent company (my dream job at the time). Her written assessment of my personality said, "Melanie's outspoken personality is too flaky to succeed in New York." I was crushed less about being rejected for the job and more about being assessed as a flake. (As a side note, three years after I moved to New York and began work at another agency, the same person who wrote that negative assessment offered me a different position at the same company. She did not remember me from the first interview.)

The idea of trying to suppress what I considered to be my authenticity in order to conform to someone else's ideals made me uncomfortable. But this happens all the time in life. There are numerous books that tell you how to dress and conduct yourself to get ahead or attract a spouse. Having interviewed and hired many job candidates in my career, I agree that you do have to look and act the role you aspire to. But you should never hide who you are out of fear that you will stand out too much. Staying true to yourself will help you fit in anywhere you go.

Embrace your authentic self! Authenticity has many characteristics. By nature of its definition, "authenticity" cannot be cookie cutter. It's your personality's DNA, and you choose the role you want it to play in your life. It's your genetic genius. It's what makes you tick and tock.

I find that people who stay true to their authenticity can do amazing things. Class clowns become successful performers. Ugly ducklings blossom into beauties without cosmetic enhancements. The nerdy computer geek becomes a tech billionaire. The bossy young girl ends up running a corporation. The inquisitive young boy becomes an investigative reporter. What seemed like an oddity earlier in life becomes a positive attribute later.

Your authenticity is both your genuineness and ingenuity. Your *genuineness* is comprised of your sincerity, honesty, and values. Your *ingenuity* makes things happen so you enjoy life more. Embrace what singles you out rather than hiding it. Put your ingenuity to work to make your uniqueness an appreciable and marketable asset rather than a distraction or disadvantage.

Makeup artists and stylists tell you to play up your best natural features. Your authenticity is your best trait. Play it up and embrace it. Much like applying makeup, embracing your authenticity entails learning to be comfortable with both perfections and imperfections. We've seen talented, beautiful people who seem to have it all fall apart because they could not handle their fame or fabulousness. Their lives may see perfect to us; but their reality is to the contrary. You need to be secure in who you are and what you have to offer and not be too self-critical.

It also means displaying that same acceptance and tolerance when dealing with others. I find many people are either intimidated or titillated by originality. Being genuine and having ingenuity will help you interact with both types of individuals, whether by making them feel comfortable or holding their interest. Ultimately, you'll find some self-centered people who will care only about how they can benefit from the experience and originality of others. Understand this and work with it instead of against it, using your ingenuity and authentic charm. Maybe it's my southern upbringing even after years living in Manhattan and dealing with some brusque people, but I find that using good manners and a sense of humor will deflect and disarm even the most difficult person. When I become argumentative or shout at someone, it goes against my authentic personality. I may be feisty at times, but never nasty. Learn to use the best of yourself to deal with the worst that may come your way, and stay true to the authentic you.

*To be yourself in a world that is constantly trying to make you something else*
*is the greatest accomplishment.*
—*Ralph Waldo Emerson, American essayist and poet*[2]

FEARLESS FABULOUS FIVE

1.  Your authenticity is what sets you apart. Make the choice to embrace it and utilize it to do and become whatever you want.

2.  Your authenticity is your calling card to open new doors and opportunities. Understand what you have to offer and make sure others appreciate it.

3.  If someone's ideal of whom you should be discredits how you feel about yourself, then that person or situation is not the ideal one for you.

4.  Be accepting of other individual's looks, strengths, and limitations. Do not be judgmental of another person's authenticity.

5.  Your authenticity does need anyone's stamp of approval.

*Authenticity is the daily practice of letting go of who we think we are*
*supposed to be and embracing who we are.*
—*Brené Brown, Author, researcher, and educator*[3]

i. b.liev'n...®

It's
Never
Too late to
Be
All
that You can
Be!

"Starting
a New
Chapter
in my Life!"

She said,
as she Confidently
Headed Off
In Pursuit of her Cause!

# Reclaim

I am not what happened to me, I am what I choose to become.

—Carl Gustav Jung,
Swiss psychiatrist and psychotherapist

# ALWAYS LOOK FOR
# AND PROJECT BRILLIANCE

*Why fit in when you were born to stand out?*
*—Unknown*

**I think we live in an era of being too judgmental. The Inter**net, where anyone can establish a blog, create a persona, and become a critic on food, fashion, entertainment, or manners fosters this culture. So does so-called reality television. Magazines criticize celebrities for being too thin or too fat. Yelpers rate everything from restaurants to dry cleaning services. We take online quizzes and surveys to see how we, and others, measure up. If we all felt we were doing all right and doing what we love, we wouldn't need to take tests or surveys to answer these questions.

We look at ourselves in the mirror and focus on our flaws instead of our best features. We size each other up based on appearance and performance rather than effort and best intentions. We evaluate people by the wrong metrics, loosely applying titles and labels.

The only label that should matter is the one *you* give to yourself. Unless you are born into royal blood, titles are simply labels we create to validate who we are. It's not the position you hold that matters—it's ultimately the purpose you have and the people you impact.

We have become our worst critics when we should be our best cheerleaders, not only for ourselves but also for those who matter to us. Instead of endlessly evaluating, we should be helping each other polish our potential and project our brilliance. Everyone has a light to shine, but sometimes it becomes dim from disuse or misuse. Sometimes you just have to clear away some mental cobwebs or emotional debris to uncover it.

Finding your brilliance may require time, effort, patience, and encouragement. If you feel your light has dulled, start fanning the flame in small ways to help it grow. Find a creative outlet. Volunteer for a local charity. Dare to try something new or return to something you gave up in the past. Embrace your quirks and idiosyncrasies. Usually there is brilliance deep inside them.

As you do this, you will learn to project your own brilliance. Practice walking into a room of people wearing a crown of confidence and flashing a smile. Identify three things about yourself that make you special and use them as your calling card to connect with people. In marketing this is called your elevator pitch—what sells who you are. Introduce yourself in a way that draws people in but does not sound pretentious. People are attracted to brilliance as long it does not outshine their own. So do it with elegance, not arrogance. And let people reflect their own brilliance back.

One of the best ways to project brilliance is to be both interesting to others and interested in what others have to say. Everyone has a story that makes them special; a good conversationalist will help bring it out. Another is to identify with a cause or a hobby or even a color. My mother is "The Purple Lady"; everything she wears is purple. She is committed to certain charities in Chattanooga where she uses her purple persona to help raise money. You don't have to be a colorful person or a clever raconteur to project brilliance. These are enhancers, special effects. Your fabulousness may be your kindness and compassion, your ability to make people laugh, or your talent for whipping up amazing cookies and cakes. It's what makes you memorable to others.

You may not feel like projecting your brilliance every day; no one wants to shine their spotlight all the time. It's like wearing a constant grin on your face. Sometimes you just need some dim-down time. But know it is there, ready to turn on and share to make you unforgettable.

*In order to be irreplaceable one must always be different.*
*—Coco Chanel, French fashion designer*[1]

## FEARLESS FABULOUS FIVE

1. Finding and projecting your brilliance will make others see you as you see yourself.

2. No one likes to be overshadowed, but many people like to be viewed in a flattering light. Learn how to shine your light on others without appearing arrogant.

3. Imitation may be the sincerest form of flattery, but originality is what will single you out.

4. What makes you unique also makes your memorable. It's your first impression and your last impression. Make it positive.

5. There may be days when you feel less than fabulous. Allow yourself time to recharge your emotional batteries.

> *Be weird. Be random. Be who you are. Because you*
> *never know who would love the person you hide.*
> —*Unknown*

# CELEBRATE THE PRIVILEGE OF AGING

*Do not regret growing older. It is a privilege denied to many.*
*—Charlie Phillips Jamaican photographer*[1]

**T**he privilege of aging. Just think about those words and their significance.

We live in a world where a high value is placed on antiques and aged wines, and where old homes and pre-war apartments carry a higher price tag. We bid high and hard for classic cars, ancient vases, vintage jewelry, and artwork by old masters.

Yet we can't bear the thought of growing old ourselves. And we are not always comfortable being around the elderly. Employers retire their older staff whether they are ready to go or not. Nursing homes are filled with the elderly whose families can no longer take care of them. An entire industry caters to making us look and feel young, and we spend a small fortune on their products each year. Remember when we spent our allowances trying to look older when we were teenagers?

We fight growing old because we live in a society where wrinkles and age spots are considered blemishes not beauty—where an elderly mind may be referred to as feeble instead of enlightened, and where employers who lead decades-old companies producing brands beloved by generations hire fresh young faces to give their own corporate image a youthful facelift. The US Congress debates Medicare and the "challenge of our aging society" as if growing old is a burden to be lifted instead of an honorable milestone.

Other cultures put a high value on aging. Respect for Elders is a national holiday in Japan, where seniors are respected for achieving age and wisdom and where asking one's age is a sign of etiquette. I would give anything to have my father and grandparents back in my life so that I could hear their voices, their time-tested knowledge, and their childhood stories.

Aging is a privilege sadly denied to those whose lives faced a premature death. It is especially hard to see a young person robbed of the right to grow old. Yet it is equally abhorrent to see people disrespect aging and waste the opportunity. We fight it with prescriptions and procedures when we should focus on staying vital and vibrant by keeping mentally and physically active. It is inevitable that with age our eyes may blur, our bones may weaken, and body parts may betray us, but we are still gifted. And we should be grateful for this.

When you face your mortality, as I did after my cancer diagnosis, having years to grow old and experience life is the gift you long for most. I now am less fearful of aging and more respectful of those whose lives stretch before me. Aging is a privilege that I embrace with more purpose and pleasure. Any young person who no longer has that privilege would agree.

Aging is a privilege to accept and embrace. Growing old means you have more years to experience life. You can take a class, learn a hobby, mentor someone, get married—or remarried. You can travel or stay home and entertain. You can do anything that your strong mind wills and your financial means allow. Being "age specific" is up to you because, as my mother likes to say, "You are as old as you feel in the day you are in." This is from a woman who celebrated her 80th birthday with a festive party in a zoo where the animals wore purple ribbons, a chorus of children sang "Happy Birthday," and guests ate purple cupcakes. It was one part fun-raiser and one part fund-raiser for a new giraffe exhibit. My mother, a perpetual partygoer, said she wanted the celebration of her life to happen while she was still living. That's the point: every year we advance should be celebrated. When the party's over, you can't dance on your grave. The art of aging gracefully is to be ageless in your attitude and timeless in your approach.

*Men grow old because they stop playing, and not conversely*
*—B. G. Stanley Hall, American psychologist and educator*[2]

## FEARLESS & FABULOUS FIVE

1. Be ageless and timeless. Don't let anyone say you are too old or too young. You can be fabulous at any age.

2. You are never too old to change your mind, change your life, or change the world.

3. Age should never be a barrier when it comes to acts of kindness or appreciation. Be considerate of anyone at any age.

4. Be curious. An active mind is your best asset for aging. You can have a childlike curiosity at any age.

5. If your outlook is ageless, your opportunities can be endless.

*When it comes to staying young, a mind-lift beats a face-lift any day.*
*—Marty Bucella, American cartoonist and illustrator*[3]

# ARE YOU LIVING
# HAPPILY EVER AFTER?

*Happily ever after does not necessarily mean perfectly ever after.*
—*Unknown*

**I have a group of friends who are all about the same age**, give or take a few years. We are all accomplished, but we have reached the point where we sometimes talk about wanting to repurpose our lives and resettle in another place. Sometimes, we find ourselves discontented with the here and now. *Here* isn't always where we feel content to live the rest of our lives. I sometimes wonder, "When, where, and how does one live 'happily ever after'?"

Many of us were encouraged to pursue a successful career, marry, raise a family, be a community citizen, and retire somewhere warm and sunny to live happily ever after. We were taught to plan for the future, invest in our children's education, and save for retirement. The truth is, many people are not going to be able to retire or may not choose to retire. We may want to hop off the traditional fast track and take a new path elsewhere. Maybe along the way, the road will have some unexpected bumps, such as unmet expectations, plans gone awry, altered attitudes, betrayals, lives irrevocably changed.

We look at ourselves and the things we've purchased: a house we now live in alone, clothes that sit in a closet waiting for those special nights out, mementoes we consider selling because they no longer seem important. We realize it's the quality of life that matters and that the sound of laughter filling the rooms makes a home far more than the four walls, roof, and floor space. The things we surround ourselves with mean nothing if they cannot be enjoyed with people we care about. The quantity of what we have does not always result in a quality life.

Friends talk about moving south to warmer climates—places where life is easier on the pocketbook and the blood pressure. They talk about moving to places with new activities to participate in and new people to meet. Is "happily ever after" always in another town? I agree that if you are not happy in a certain place, career, or relationship, you should move on. But make sure when you move on, it's not to run away, but rather to move forward.

Take out a piece of paper and make a list of everything that makes you happy. Then check off everything on that list that is currently in your life. Then look at what is not checked off and decide, "What is the one thing I can I do this year to make this happen?" Finally, make a second list of the happiness you can bring to others and check off one thing you can do to make someone else's life more pleasant.

I think "happily ever after" is elusive. It's not an end result; it's a state of being. It's not only the destination but the routes you take. I also think we need to give and share happiness to find it in ourselves. Instead of seeking happiness, we need to sow the seeds ourselves and bring the garden wherever we go. Happiness tends to bloom from positive thoughts, and it's nurtured through kind actions and drops of laughter.

The "happily ever after" of our childhood books is not necessarily the modern narrative of our lives. We don't live in fairy tales; we live in reality. But we have the ability to be the author of our own story, and how we want the chapters to unfold is our choice.

*When I was 5 years old, my mother always told me that happiness was the key to life. When I went to school, they asked me what I wanted to be when I grew up. I wrote down 'happy'. They told me I didn't understand the assignment, and I told them they didn't understand life.*
*—Unknown*

FEARLESS FABULOUS FIVE

1.  Happily ever after is a myth. Instead, focus on being happy in the present moment.

2.  Happiness is not just about where you are physically but also about where you are mentally and spiritually. It is not as much about who you're with as it is who you believe you are. It is both your why and your why not to living.

3. Happiness is keeping your mind open and your outlook positive and keeping negative thoughts and energy out.

4. You may not be happy every hour of every day. But try to do something that makes you smile and feel good every day. Snack on laughter, not chips.

5. If you find yourself actually living happily ever after, please remember to share your good fortune!

*If you look at what you have in your life, you will always have more. If you look at what you don't have in life, you will never have enough.*
*—Oprah Winfrey*[1]

# HAVING THE LAST WORD

*The bitterest tears shed over graves are for words left unsaid
and deeds left undone.*
—Harriet Beecher Stowe, American author and abolitionist[1]

**W**e've all heard the term *famous last words*. But what about having the final word?

My friend and author of *Sexy After Cancer*, Barbara Musser, wrote an article whose words resonated with me. She said, "Had I known that my last conversation with my mother was the final one before her sudden death, I would have chosen to say other things to her."[2]

It's ironic how when I write, I choose my words carefully, but when I address people in my life who matter, I'm careless. Do you do this? Do you brush someone off when they call? Do you nag a spouse, criticize someone through offhanded remarks, or speak sharply to someone when you feel rushed or stressed? Do you listen and think before you reply? Do you *really* listen, or are you just half-listening while multitasking?

I was taught to count to ten before replying to anyone. I was also taught to count to ten to control my anger. Those ten seconds of attitude adjustment are what many of us need to practice more often.

My mother told me that every night, she and my father would have the same exchange. One would say, "I love you." The other would respond, "I love you more." These were their final words to each other before Dad died in his sleep.

My final words with my father were strong and positive because I knew he was dying and that I would never see him again. I shudder to think of how I would have felt if he had died suddenly and our final words had been acrimonious. I learned from the experience there are never enough words to express your gratitude and love for someone and it is shame to leave it to the end. Don't hold back telling someone how much they mean to you. Such words left unsaid are wasted.

What we say matters. What we don't say matters too. Silence can be as powerful as speaking aloud. I've learned that using the right language and a friendly tone of voice are great currency to use to open doors, connect with people around the world, disarm confrontations, and make others feels better. Language and how you communicate can either be a bridge or a barrier.

Listening with intent is as important as speaking your thoughts. Sometimes, if you feel you have nothing to say, be a better listener to the person you are with. Ask questions. People will think you're a brilliant conversationalist if you give them the chance to talk. An unknown author once said, "Speak in such a way that others listen to you. Listen in ways that others love to speak to you."

It is also important to get things off your chest rather than let emotions simmer inside until they reach a boiling point. Silence is not golden if it is repressing your true voice. If something is weighing on your mind, be your own advocate and express your concern. Saying your piece will bring you peace of mind. And it is better to speak a truth than to be false to yourself.

We should choose the words we say as carefully as we choose anything else that matters in our lives. Like a bad post on social media or a poorly written memo, words can deliver the wrong message that, even once retracted, still linger in the memory

Words are powerful tools. They can build and strengthen or weaken and destroy. They can make an impression that can last forever.

*Be sure to taste your words before you spit them out.*
*—Unknown*

FEARLESS FABULOUS FIVE

1.  It's better to speak your mind than to let things fester, but choose your words carefully and understand their consequences.

2.  It's better to choose words that help than words that hurt. Use words to turn unjust actions into positive changes.

3.  Asking questions to get better answers is smarter than remaining silent.

4. Never begin or end the day with a negative thought or negative words.

5. If the *cat has your tongue,* express yourself in writing or in a gesture that says what you mean. As you've heard before, actions speak louder than words.

*Always tell someone how you feel, because opportunities are lost in the blink of an eye, but regrets can last for a lifetime.*
—*Carson Kolhoff*[3]

# IT IS NEVER TOO LATE
# TO START OVER

*Though no one can go back and make a new start, anyone*
*can start from now and make a new ending.*
*—Carl Bard, American academic*[1]

**R**einvention is a popular theme these days. Women and men often rethink their lives and the legacy they want to leave. People reinvent their lives for many reasons. Sometimes it is by choice: the life choices you made are no longer fulfilling, and you desire change. Sometimes it is by economic necessity: you lose your job or close your business. Reinvention may result from a personal challenge, such as divorce, the death of a loved one, or a health issue. The need or desire to make a change can happen at any age or stage of your life.

For many people, myself included, a life-changing occurrence is the tipping point in the process of one's reinvention. My decision was to live a life with less stress, more pleasure, greater purpose, more time to enjoy today, and less worry about tomorrow. I wanted to repurpose the skills in my toolbox in new ways, and I wanted to remain healthy. This required a sizeable mental adjustment. I had to learn to place fewer demands on myself, live with less, stop competing with others, and stop comparing my old life to my new life.

But through it all, I learned that it is never too late to start over. Even if you have made bad decisions and wrong choices, you can start fresh. You just have to believe that you can do it, and you can make it happen. You can start over at twenty, fifty, seventy, or older. My mother-in-law became a wardrobe consultant in her seventies after she was widowed. My mother had several reinventions. She started out as a speech therapist, later sold life insurance, then became a newspaper columnist, taught as an adjunct professor in public speaking at the University of Tennessee in Chattanooga, and also served on the boards of several charitable organizations.

If you are restarting a career or reentering the work force, you may need to repurpose your skills and repackage your presentation. You may need to pursue a new path of education or training. Take courses at a local college. Find a mentor. Volunteer. Whatever you decide to do, fine-tune your skills and be prepared to move sideways in order to move forward.

If you are starting over after a bad relationship, you need to discard negative feelings from your old life. How can you fill your life with new joy if you're still overloaded with anger? If you carry too much emotional baggage, you will not have the space in your heavy heart to allow someone in.

Reinvention takes patience. It is a process, not a happening. Reinvention is the route you take to get to a new destination in your life. And if the direction you choose hits a dead end, start over again. Being fearless and fabulous on your terms means knowing when to make the best decisions at the right time for you.

> *If you don't like the road you're walking, start paving another one.*
> —*Dolly Parton, Country music singer, songwriter, and actress*[2]

FEARLESS FABULOUS FIVE

1. Know why you're starting over, and make sure it's for the right reason: making a difference in your life, not making an escape plan.
2. Unlock any emotional chains that may hold you back. You need to be unfettered by anxiety, resentment, and regret if you are to start over.
3. It's good to aim high, but be realistic about how long it may take, and be patient. Starting over should not be a race to the finish line. It should about walking a better path.
4. Find a mentor or coach to help you along the way. It's a great investment.
5. If you find the direction you are heading is leading to a dead end, switch directions.

> *No matter how hard the past you can always begin again.*
> —*Jack Kornfield, American author and teacher*[3]

# FEARLESS, FABULOUS YOU! WHAT'S YOUR STORY?

At the end of the day, the only questions I will ask of myself will be:

*Did I laugh enough?*
*Did I love enough?*
*Did I make a difference*
*—Author Unknown*


# RECHARGE

I WILL MAKE ME A PRIORITY BY:

1.

2.

3.

4.

5.


THE THINGS IN MY LIFE THAT BRING ME JOY:

1.

2.

3.

4.

5.

# RELEASE

I AM D.W.D. (DONE WITH DWELLING) ON:

1.
2.
3.
4.
5.

I AM GOING TO STEP OUT OF MY COMFORT ZONE BY:

1.
2.
3.
4.
**5.**

# RECONNECT

MY BEST TOOLS ARE:

1.
2.
3.
4.
5.

I AM GRATEFUL FOR:

1.
2.
3.
4.
5.

# RECLAIM

I AM GOING TO START:

1.
2.
3.
4.
5.

THE FIVE THINGS I WANT TO BE REMEMBERED FOR:

1.
2.
3.
4.
5.

# NOTES

FRONT MATTER

Anna Taylor, *The Angels' Voice*, accessed September 10, 2014, http://www.anna-taylor.co.uk/.

RECHARGE

John O'Donohue, "Crossing Thresholds," December 29, 2012, http://www.johnodonohue.com/crossing-thresholds.

CHAPTER 1

1. Kelly Angard, "taking notes," April 1, 2009, accessed September 10, 2014, http://kellyangard.com/gallery/bodyscapes-gallery/.

2. Hillel, *Pirqe Aboth*, trans. Charles Taylor, 1:14, accessed September 10, 2014. http://www.sacred-texts.com/jud/sjf/sjf03.htm.

CHAPTER 2

1. Dr. Wayne W. Dyer, "The Motivational Speakers Hall of Fame," accessed September 10, 2014, http://getmotivation.com/drwdyer.htm.

2. Virginia Satir, quoted in goodreads.com, accessed September 10, 2014, http://www.goodreads.com/author/quotes/312508.Virginia_Satir.

3. Eleanor Roosevelt, freestanding quotation, *The Reader's Digest Association*, September 1940, 37:84.

CHAPTER 3

1. Oprah Winfrey, O Magazine, April 2003.

2. Amy Rubin Flett, "More Life," pinwheeldesigns Etsy Shop, https://www.etsy.com/people/pinwheeldesigns.

3. Swedish Proverb, in *Words of Wellness*, ed. Joseph Sutton (Carlsbad: Hay House, 1991).

## CHAPTER 4

1. *The Free Dictionary*, s.v. "lean in," accessed September 10, 2014, http://idioms.thefreedictionary.com/lean+in.

2. Booker T. Washington, The Booker T. Washington Society, accessed September 10, 2014, http://www.btwsociety.org/library/misc/quotes.php.

## CHAPTER 5

1. Lupita Nyong'o, acceptance speech, 7th Annual Black Women in Hollywood, February 28, 2014, *Essence Magazine*, http://www.essence.com/2014/02/27/lupita-nyongo-delivers-moving-black-women-hollywood-acceptance-speech/.

2. Amy Rubin Flett, "need fixing," pinwheeldesigns Etsy Shop, https://www.etsy.com/shop/pinwheeldesigns/sold?page=1.

## RELEASE

Jack Kornfield, Buddha's Little Instruction Book, (New York: Bantam Books, 1996).

## CHAPTER 6

1. James Baldwin, quoted in *Wisdom for the Soul: Five Millennia of Prescriptions for Spiritual Healing*, ed. Larry Chang, (Washington, DC: Gnosophia, 2006).

2. Mary Engelbreit, "If You Don't Like Something," accessed September 11, 2014, http://www.maryengelbreit.com/store/If-You-Don-t-Like-Something-Fine-Print.html.

3. Jim Rohn, quoted in lifechangequotes.com, accessed September 11, 2014, http://lifechangequotes.com/jim-rohn-quote-change/.

## CHAPTER 7

1. Hermann Hesse, quoted in goodreads.com, accessed September 11, 2014, http://www.goodreads.com/author/quotes/1113469.Hermann_Hesse.

2. Barbara De Angelis, quoted in selfgrowth.com, accessed September 11, 2014, http://www.selfgrowth.com/experts/barbara_de_angelis.html.

## CHAPTER 8

1. Thomas A. Richards, "Positive Thoughts To Dwell On," The Anxiety Network, accessed September 11, 2014, http://anxietynetwork.com/content/positive-thoughts.

2. *Merriam-Webster Online*, s.v. "regret," accessed September 11, 2014,

http://www.merriam-webster.com/dictionary/regret.

3. Seneca the younger, quoted in G. Shawn Hunter *Out Think: How Innovative Leaders Drive Exceptional Outcomes* (Hoboken: Wiley, 2013).

4. Helen Keller, quoted in examiner.com, June 27, 2011, accessed September 11, 2014, http://www.examiner.com/article/helen-keller-quotes-to-celebrate-helen-keller-s-birthday.

CHAPTER 9

1. *The Free Dictionary*, s.v. "pride," accessed September 11, 2014, http://www.thefreedictionary.com/Pride.

2. Proverbs 16:18 (King James Version).

3. Ezra Taft Benson, quoted in "A Mighty Change of Heart," *Ensign,* November 1993, https://www.lds.org/ensign/print/1993/11/a-mighty-change-of-heart?lang=eng&clang=eng.

CHAPTER 10

1. John Augustus Shedd, *Salt from My Attic* (Portland: Mosher, 1928).

2. Katherine Hepburn and Susan Crimp, *Katharine Hepburn Once Said . . . : Great Lines to Live By,* (New York: HarperCollins, 2003), 30.

RECONNECT

Reba McEntire, accessed September 12, 2014, https://www.goodreads.com/quotes/132414-to-succeed-in-life-you-need-three-things-a-wishbone.

CHAPTER 11

1. George Lucas, quoted in "Your Morning Shot: George Lucas," *GQ*, March 26, 2012, http://www.gq.com/style/blogs/the-gq-eye/2012/03/your-morning-shot-george-lucas.html.

2. Henry van Dyke, quoted in "Handicapped Individuals Services and Training Act: hearing before the subcommittee on Select Education of the Committee on Education and Labor, House of Representatives, Ninety-seventh Congress second session, on HR 6820 . . . hearing held in St. Paul, MN, and Loretto, MN, on September 2, 1982," 223.

3. Mark Twain, "Friday, February 23, 1906," *Autobiography of Mark Twain*, ed. Harriet Elinor Smith (Berkeley: Mark Twain Project, 2010), 1:376.

CHAPTER 12

1. Steve Jobs, "How To Live before You Die" (Stanford University commencement speech, June 2005), http://news.stanford.edu/news/2005/june15/jobs-061505.html.

2. Vincent Van Gogh, quoted in goodreads.com, accessed September 12, 2014, https://www.goodreads.com/author/quotes/34583.Vincent_van_Gogh.

3. George Bernard Shaw, quoted in goodreads.com, accessed September 12, 2014, https://www.goodreads.com/quotes/8727-life-isn-t-about-finding-yourself-life-is-about-creating-yourself.

CHAPTER 13

1. Mary Kay Ash, quoted in goodreads.com, accessed September 12, 2014. http://www.goodreads.com/quotes/394694-for-every-failure-there-s-an-alternative-course-of-action-you

2. Orinn Woodward and Chris Brady, *LIFE: Living Intentionally for Excellence* (Market Place Flint: Obstacles Press, 2011).

CHAPTER 14

1. Allen Saunders, *Readers Digest Magazine*, January 1957.

2. *English Word Information*, s.v. "Serendipity," accessed September 12, 2014, http://wordinfo.info/unit/1941/s:by.

3. Vivian Greene, accessed September 12, 2014, http://www.viviangreene.com/.

4. Lawrence Block, quoted in Mina Parker *Silver Linings: Meditations on Finding Joy and Beauty in Unexpected Places* (Newburyport: Conari Press, 2008).

CHAPTER 15

1. Dr. Christina Hibbert, "10 Benefits of Practicing Gratitude," *the psychologist, the mom, & me* (blog), November 17, 2012, accessed September 12, 2014, http://www.drchristinahibbert.com/10-benefits-of-practicing-gratitude/.

2. William Arthur Ward, quoted in Allen Klein, *Change Your Life!* (Berkeley: Viva Editions, 2010)

3. A. A. Milne, *Winnie-the-Pooh* (New York: Dutton Children's Books, 2001, first published 1926).

REFRAME

Ayn Rand, *Fountainhead* (New York: Signet, 1996).

CHAPTER 16

1. Elizabeth Edwards, quoted in "Elizabeth Edwards: What Will Be Her Greatest Legacy?" ABC News, December 8, 2010, accessed September 13, 2014,

## NOTES

story?id=12341421.

2. Barry Neil Kaufman, *Happiness is a Choice* (New York: Ballantine, 2011).

CHAPTER 17

1. *Merriam-Webster Online*, s.v. "success," accessed September 13, 2014,
http://www.merriam-webster.com/dictionary/success.

2. *Merriam-Webster Online*, s.v. "achievement," accessed September 13, 2014,
http://www.merriam-webster.com/dictionary/achievement.

3. Helen Hayes, quoted in *Words of Wellness: A Treasury of Quotations for Well-
Being*, ed. Joseph Sutton (Carlsbad: Hay House, 2014).

4. Online College, "Famous Failures Who Later Succeeded," compiled by site
administrator, February 16, 2010, accessed September 13, 2014, http://
www.onlinecollege.org/2010/02/16/50-famously-successful-people-who-
failed-at-first/.

CHAPTER 18

1. William Feather, quoted in Stephen R. Covey *Everyday Greatness: Inspiration for a Meaningful Life* (Nashville: Thomas Nelson, 2006).

2. His Holiness the Dalai Lama, quoted in goodreads.com, accessed September 13, 2014, http://www.goodreads.com/author/quotes/570218.
Dalai_Lama_XIV.

CHAPTER 19

1. Marcel Proust, *La Prisonnière*, English translation (1923).

2. H. Jackson Brown Jr., *P.S. I Love You* (Nashville: Thomas Nelson, 1990).

3. Les Brown, quoted in : Amy Herring, *Astrology of the Moon : An Illuminating
Journey Through the Signs and Houses* (Woodbury, MN : Llewellyn Publications,
2010).

CHAPTER 20

1. Judy Garland, quoted in Dayanara Torres, *Married to Me: How Committing
to Myself Led to Triumph After Divorce* (New York: Celebra, 2008).

2. Ralph Waldo Emerson, quoted in Joyce Meyer, *100 Ways to Simplify Your
Life* (New York: Hachette Book Group, 2007).

3. Brené Brown, *The Gifts of Imperfection: Let Go of Who You Think You're Supposed to Be and Embrace Who You Are* (Center City, MN: Hazelden, 2010).

Reclaim

C.G. Jung, quoted in: James Hollis, *On This Journey We Call Life: Living the Questions*, (Toronto: Inner City Books, 2003).

Chapter 21

1.  Coco Chanel, quoted in: Marcel Haedrich, *Coco Chanel: Her Life, Her Secrets*, (New York: Little, Brown and Company, 1971).

Chapter 22

1.  Charlie Phillips, quoted in fmsreliability.com, accessed September 15, 2014, http://www.fmsreliability.com/publishing/rqotd-79/.

2.  G. Stanley Hall, *Adolescence: Its Psychology and Its Relations to Physiology, Anthropology, Sociology, Sex, Crime, Religion and Education*, (New York: D. Appleton and Company, 1904).

3.  Marty Bucella, as quoted in: Jack Canfield, Mark Victor Hansen, and Amy Newmark, *Chicken Soup for the Soul: Inspiration for the Young at Heart*, (New York: Chicken Soup for the Soul Publishing, 2011).

Chapter 23

1.  Oprah Winfrey, quoted in Joan Garrett, *The Journey Continues: Life's Travel Guide for Teens and Young Adults*, (Bloomington: iUniverse, 2010).

Chapter 24

1.  Harriet Beecher Stowe, *Little Foxes*, (Boston: Fields, Osgood, and Co., 1869).

2.  Barbara Musser, "Sexy Heart Broken Open," *Sexy After Cancer*, February 10, 2014, accessed September 11, 2014, http://www.sexyaftercancer.com/sexy-blog/heart-broken-open/

3.  Carson Kolhoff, SearchQuote.com, accessed September 11, 2014, http://www.searchquotes.com/quotation/Always_tell_someone_how_you_feel,_because_opportunities_are_lost_in_the_blink_of_an_eye_but_regret_c/327409/.

Chapter 25

1.  Carl Bard, quoted in Brenda Bence, *Master the Brand Called YOU*, (Las Vegas: Global Insight Communications, 2014).

2.  Dolly Parton, quoted in: Paula Munier, *On Being Blonde: Wit and Wisdom from the World's Most Infamous Blondes*, (Gloucester, MA: Fair Winds Press, 2004).

3.  Jack Kornfield, quoted in Mary Mann, *Science and Spirituality*, (Bloomington, IN: AuthorHouse, 2004).

# ABOUT THE AUTHOR

*The worth of a woman is not the sum of her body parts but the amount of effort she makes to find purpose, the accumulation of wisdom she earns and shares with others, and the values she has in her heart.*
—Melanie Young

Photo: Jennifer Mitchell Photography

**M**elanie Young knows how to face challenges with grit, grace, and wit and reframe them to make things happen for the better. She is a motivational muse for reinvention who wants to inspire anyone who feels stuck and wants to make a change. After surviving breast cancer, she changed how she wanted to live her life. She committed to focusing on inspiration over aspiration by helping others make better and healthier choices to enjoy life on their terms. Her first book, *Getting Things Off My Chest: A Survivor's Guide to Staying Fearless & Fabulous in the Face of Breast Cancer,* helps newly-diagnosed cancer patients stay focused and make smarter choices about caring for their well-being during and after treatment. The book received the 2014 International Book Award for cancer health topics. She is an active speaker and advocate for women's health, education, and empowerment and shares her insights on her blog, *Getting Things Off My Chest*, in her numerous articles and speeches, and on her radio show "Fearless, Fabulous You!" on W4WN—the Women-4-Women Network. Melanie turned her passions for wine, food, connecting people, and supporting inspirational causes into a successful marketing and events business, The Connected Table®, and cohosts a national radio show by the same name with her husband, David Ransom. During her culinary career, she developed, launched, and managed the James Beard Foundation Awards and New York Restaurant Week.

Born and raised in Chattanooga, Tennessee, she now resides in New York's Hudson Valley.

You can follow Melanie at:
*www.melanieyoung.com* and *Twitter@mightymelanie*